FEMA 308

REPAIR OF EARTHQUAKE DAMAGED CONCRETE AND MASONRY WALL BUILDINGS

Prepared by:

The Applied Technology Council

555 Twin Dolphin Drive, Suite 550
Redwood City, California 94065

Prepared for:

The Partnership for Response and Recovery

Washington, D.C.

Funded by:

Federal Emergency Management Agency

1998

Applied Technology Council

The Applied Technology Council (ATC) is a nonprofit, tax-exempt corporation established in 1971 through the efforts of the Structural Engineers Association of California. ATC is guided by a Board of Directors consisting of representatives appointed by the American Society of Civil Engineers, the Structural Engineers Association of California, the Western States Council of Structural Engineers Associations, and four at-large representatives concerned with the practice of structural engineering. Each director serves a three-year term.

The purpose of ATC is to assist the design practitioner in structural engineering (and related design specialty fields such as soils, wind, and earthquake) in the task of keeping abreast of and effectively using technological developments. ATC also identifies and encourages needed research and develops consensus opinions on structural engineering issues in a nonproprietary format. ATC thereby fulfills a unique role in funded information transfer.

Project management and administration are carried out by a full-time Executive Director and support staff. Project work is conducted by a wide range of highly qualified consulting professionals, thus incorporating the experience of many individuals from academia, research, and professional practice who would not be available from any single organization. Funding for ATC projects is obtained from government agencies and from the private sector in the form of tax-deductible contributions.

1998-1999 Board of Directors

Notice

This report was prepared under Contract EMW-95-C-4685 between the Federal Emergency Management Agency and the Partnership for Response and Recovery.

Any opinions, findings, conclusions, or recommendations expressed in this publication do not necessarily reflect the views of the Applied Technology Council (ATC), the Partnership for Response and Recovery (PaRR), or the Federal Emergency Management Agency (FEMA). Additionally, neither ATC, PaRR, FEMA, nor any of their employees makes any warranty, expressed or implied, nor assumes any legal liability or responsibility for the accuracy, completeness, or usefulness of any information, product, or process included in this publication. Users of information from this publication assume all liability arising from such use.

For further information concerning this document or the activities of the ATC, contact the Executive Director, Applied Technolgy Council, 555 Twin Dolphin Drive, Suite 550, Redwood City, California 94065; phone 650-595-1542; fax 650-593-2320; e-mail atc@atcouncil.org.

Preface

Following the two damaging California earthquakes in 1989 (Loma Prieta) and 1994 (Northridge), many concrete wall and masonry wall buildings were repaired using federal disaster assistance funding. The repairs were based on inconsistent criteria, giving rise to controversy regarding criteria for the repair of cracked concrete and masonry wall buildings. To help resolve this controversy, the Federal Emergency Management Agency (FEMA) initiated a project on evaluation and repair of earthquake-damaged concrete and masonry wall buildings in 1996. The project was conducted through the Partnership for Response and Recovery (PaRR), a joint venture of Dewberry & Davis of Fairfax, Virginia, and Woodward-Clyde Federal Services of Gaithersburg, Maryland. The Applied Technology Council (ATC), under subcontract to PaRR, was responsible for developing technical criteria and procedures (the ATC-43 project).

The ATC-43 project addresses the investigation and evaluation of earthquake damage and discusses policy issues related to the repair and upgrade of earthquake-damaged buildings. The project deals with buildings whose primary lateral-force-resisting systems consist of concrete or masonry bearing walls with flexible or rigid diaphragms, or whose vertical-load-bearing systems consist of concrete or steel frames with concrete or masonry infill panels. The intended audience is design engineers, building owners, building regulatory officials, and government agencies.

The project results are reported in three documents. The FEMA 306 report, *Evaluation of Earthquake Damaged Concrete and Masonry Wall Buildings, Basic Procedures Manual,* provides guidance on evaluating damage and analyzing future performance. Included in the document are component damage classification guides, and test and inspection guides. FEMA 307, *Evaluation of Earthquake Damaged Concrete and Masonry Wall Buildings, Technical Resources,* contains supplemental information including results from a theoretical analysis of the effects of prior damage on single-degree-of-freedom mathematical models, additional background information on the component guides, and an example of the application of the basic procedures. FEMA 308, *The Repair of Earthquake Damaged Concrete and Masonry Wall Buildings,* discusses the policy issues pertaining to the repair of earthquake-damaged buildings and illustrates how the procedures developed for the project can be used to provide a technically sound basis for policy decisions. It also provides guidance for the repair of damaged components.

The project also involved a workshop to provide an opportunity for the user community to review and comment on the proposed evaluation and repair criteria. The workshop, open to the profession at large, was held in Los Angeles on June 13, 1997 and was attended by 75 participants.

The project was conducted under the direction of ATC Senior Consultant Craig Comartin, who served as Co-Principal Investigator and Project Director. Technical and management direction were provided by a Technical Management Committee consisting of Christopher Rojahn (Chair), Craig Comartin (Co-Chair), Daniel Abrams, Mark Doroudian, James Hill, Jack Moehle, Andrew Merovich (ATC Board Representative), and Tim McCormick. The Technical Management Committee created two Issue Working Groups to pursue directed research to document the state of the knowledge in selected key areas: (1) an Analysis Working Group, consisting of Mark Aschheim (Group Leader) and Mete Sozen (Senior Consultant) and (2) a Materials Working Group, consisting of Joe Maffei (Group Leader and Reinforced Concrete Consultant), Greg Kingsley (Reinforced Masonry Consultant), Bret Lizundia (Unreinforced Masonry Consultant), John Mander (Infilled Frame Consultant), Brian Kehoe and other consultants from Wiss, Janney, Elstner and Associates (Tests, Investigations, and Repairs Consultant). A Project Review Panel provided technical overview and guidance. The Panel members were Gregg Borchelt, Gene Corley, Edwin Huston, Richard Klingner, Vilas Mujumdar, Hassan Sassi, Carl Schulze, Daniel Shapiro, James Wight, and Eugene Zeller. Nancy Sauer and Peter Mork provided technical editing and report production services, respectively. Affiliations are provided in the list of project participants.

The Applied Technology Council and the Partnership for Response and Recovery gratefully acknowledge the cooperation and insight provided by the FEMA Technical Monitor, Robert D. Hanson.

Tim McCormick
PaRR Task Manager

Christopher Rojahn
ATC-43 Principal Investigator
ATC Executive Director

Table of Contents

List of Figures

List of Tables

List of Repair Guides

(See Section 4.3.3)

Prologue

This document is one of three to result from the ATC-43 project funded by the Federal Emergency Management Agency (FEMA). The goal of the project is to develop technically sound procedures to evaluate the effects of earthquake damage on buildings with primary lateral-force-resisting systems consisting of concrete or masonry bearing walls or infilled frames. They are based on the knowledge derived from research and experience in engineering practice regarding the performance of these types of buildings and their components. The procedures require thoughtful examination and review prior to implementation. The ATC-43 project team strongly urges individual users to read all of the documents carefully to form an overall understanding of the damage evaluation procedures and repair techniques.

Before this project, formalized procedures for the investigation and evaluation of earthquake-damaged buildings were limited to those intended for immediate use in the field to identify potentially hazardous conditions. ATC-20, *Procedures for Postearthquake Safety Evaluation of Buildings*, and its addendum, ATC-20-2 (ATC, 1989 and 1995) are the definitive documents for this purpose. Both have proven to be extremely useful in practical applications. ATC-20 recognizes and states that in many cases, detailed structural engineering evaluations are required to investigate the implications of earthquake damage and the need for repairs. This project provides a framework and guidance for those engineering evaluations.

What have we learned?

The project team for ATC-43 began its work with a thorough review of available analysis techniques, field observations, test data, and emerging evaluation and design methodologies. The first objective was to understand the effects of damage on future building performance. The main points are summarized below.

- **Component behavior controls global performance.**

Recently developed guidelines for structural engineering seismic analysis and design techniques focus on building displacement rather than forces as the primary parameter for the characterization of seismic performance. This approach models the building as an assembly of its individual components. Force-deformation properties (e.g., elastic stiffness, yield point, ductility) control the behavior of wall panels, beams, columns, and other components. The component behavior, in turn, governs the overall displacement of the building and its seismic performance. Thus, the evaluation of the effects of damage on building performance must concentrate on how component properties change as a result of damage.

- **Indicators of damage (e.g., cracking, spalling) are meaningful only in light of the mode of component behavior.**

Damage affects the behavior of individual components differently. Some exhibit ductile modes of post-elastic behavior, maintaining strength even with large displacements. Others are brittle and lose strength abruptly after small inelastic displacements. The post-elastic behavior of a structural component is a function of material properties, geometric proportions, details of construction, and the combination of demand actions (axial, flexural, shearing, torsional) imposed upon it. As earthquake shaking imposes these actions on components, the components tend to exhibit predominant modes of behavior as damage occurs. For example, if earthquake shaking and its associated inertial forces and frame distortions cause a reinforced concrete wall panel to rotate at each end, with in-plane distortion, statics defines the relationship between the associated bending moments and shear force. The behavior of the panel depends on its strength in flexure relative to that in shear. Cracks and other signs of damage must be interpreted in the context of the mode of component behavior. A one-eighth-inch crack in a wall panel on the verge of brittle shear failure is a very serious condition. The same size crack in a flexurally-controlled panel may be insignificant with regard to future seismic performance. This is, perhaps, the most important finding of the ATC-43 project: the significance of cracks and other signs of damage, with respect to the future performance of a building, depends on the mode of behavior of the components in which the damage is observed.

- **Damage may reveal component behavior that differs from that predicted by evaluation and design methodologies.**

When designing a building or evaluating an undamaged building, engineers rely on theory and their own experience to visualize how earthquakes will affect the structure. The same is true when they evaluate the effects of actual damage after an earthquake, with one important difference. If engineers carefully observe the nature and extent of the signs of the damage, they can greatly enhance their insight into the way the building actually responded to earthquake shaking. Sometimes the actual behavior differs from that predicted using design equations or procedures. This is not really surprising, since design procedures must account conservatively for a wide range of uncertainty in material properties, behavior parameters, and ground shaking characteristics. Ironically, actual damage during an earthquake has the potential for improving the engineer's knowledge of the behavior of the building. When considering the effects of damage on future performance, this knowledge is important.

- **Damage may not significantly affect displacement demand in future larger earthquakes.**

One of the findings of the ATC-43 project is that prior earthquake damage does not affect maximum displacement response in future, larger earthquakes in many instances. At first, this may seem illogical. Observing a building with cracks in its walls after an earthquake and visualizing its future performance in an even larger event, it is natural to assume that it is worse off than if the damage had not occurred. It seems likely that the maximum displacement in the future, larger earthquake would be greater than if it had not been damaged. Extensive nonlinear time-history analyses performed for the project indicated otherwise for many structures. This was particularly true in cases in which significant strength degradation did not occur during the prior, smaller earthquake. Careful examination of the results revealed that maximum displacements in time histories of relatively large earthquakes tended to occur after the loss of stiffness and strength would have taken place even in an undamaged structure. In other words, the damage that occurs in a prior,

smaller event would have occurred early in the subsequent, larger event anyway.

What does it mean?

The ATC-43 project team has formulated performance-based procedures for evaluating the effects of damage. These can be used to quantify losses and to develop repair strategies. The application of these procedures has broad implications.

- **Performance-based damage evaluation uses the actual behavior of a building, as evidenced by the observed damage, to identify specific deficiencies.**

The procedures focus on the connection between damage and component behavior and the implications for estimating actual behavior in future earthquakes. This approach has several important benefits. First, it provides a meaningful engineering basis for measuring the effects of damage. It also identifies performance characteristics of the building in its pre-event and damaged states. The observed damage itself is used to calibrate the analysis and to improve the building model. For buildings found to have unacceptable damage, the procedures identify specific deficiencies at a component level, thereby facilitating the development of restoration or upgrade repairs.

- **Performance-based damage evaluation provides an opportunity for better allocation of resources.**

The procedures themselves are technical engineering tools. They do not establish policy or prescribe rules for the investigation and repair of damage. They may enable improvements in both private and public policy, however. In past earthquakes, decisions on what to do about damaged buildings have been hampered by a lack of technical procedures to evaluate the effects of damage and repairs. It has also been difficult to investigate the risks associated with various repair alternatives. The framework provided by performance-based damage evaluation procedures can help to remove some of these roadblocks. In the long run, the procedures may tend to reduce the prevailing focus on the loss caused by damage from its pre-event conditions and to increase the focus on what the damage reveals about future building performance. It makes little sense to implement unnecessary repairs to buildings that would perform relatively well even in a damaged condition. Nor is it wise to neglect buildings in which the component behavior reveals serious hazards regardless of the extent of damage.

- **Engineering judgment and experience are essential to the successful application of the procedures.**

ATC-20 and its addendum, ATC-20-2, were developed to be used by individuals who might be somewhat less knowledgeable about earthquake building performance than practicing structural engineers. In contrast, the detailed investigation of damage using the performance-based procedures of this document and the companion FEMA 306 report (ATC, 1998a) and FEMA 307 report (ATC, 1998b) must be implemented by an experienced engineer. Although the documents include information in concise formats to facilitate field operations, they must not be interpreted as a "match the pictures" exercise for unqualified observers. Use of these guideline materials requires a thorough understanding of the underlying theory and empirical justifications contained in the documents. Similarly, the use of the simplified direct method to estimate losses has limitations. The decision to use this method and the interpretation of the results must be made by an experienced engineer.

- **The new procedures are different from past damage evaluation techniques and will continue to evolve in the future.**

The technical basis of the evaluation procedures is essentially that of the emerging performance-based seismic and structural design procedures. These will take some time to be assimilated in the engineering community. The same is true for building officials. Seminars, workshops, and training sessions are required not only to introduce and explain the procedures but also to gather feedback and to improve the overall process. Additionally, future materials-testing and analytical research will enhance the basic framework developed for this project. Current project documents are initial editions to be revised and improved over the years.

In addition to the project team, a Project Review Panel has reviewed the damage evaluation and repair procedures and each of the three project documents. This group of experienced practitioners, researchers, regulators, and materials industry representatives reached a unanimous consensus that the products are technically sound and that they represent the state of knowledge on the evaluation and repair of earthquake-damaged concrete and masonry wall buildings. At the same time, all who contributed to this project acknowledge that the recommendations depart from traditional practices. Owners, design professionals, building officials, researchers, and all others with an interest in the performance of buildings during earthquakes are encouraged to review these documents and to contribute to their continued improvement and enhancement. Use of the documents should provide realistic assessments of the effects of damage and valuable insight into the behavior of structures during earthquakes. In the long run, they hopefully will contribute to sensible private and public policy regarding earthquake-damaged buildings.

1. Introduction

1.1 Purpose

The purpose of this document is to present practical guidance for the repair and upgrading of earthquake-damaged buildings with primary lateral-force-resisting systems consisting of concrete bearing walls, masonry bearing walls, or infilled frames. The guidance consists of a policy framework for facilitating the determination of the appropriate scope of repair or upgrading measures. This document also includes outlines of specific repair techniques that can address the component damage common to these buildings. The criteria and procedures are based on the evaluation of the anticipated seismic performance of a subject building at three different times: in its condition immediately before the damaging earthquake (pre-event), in its damaged condition, and in its repaired or upgraded condition. This document may be used as a technical resource to facilitate the settlement of insurance claims, the development of policy and strategy for repair, or other appropriate purposes. The intended users of the document are design engineers, building owners, building officials, insurance adjusters, and government agencies.

1.2 Scope

This document is one of several to result from a research project on the evaluation and repair of earthquake-damaged concrete and masonry wall buildings. Concrete and masonry wall buildings include those with vertical-load-bearing wall panels, with and without intermediate openings. In this document, concrete and masonry wall buildings also include those with vertical-load-bearing frames of concrete or steel that incorporate masonry or concrete infill panels to resist horizontal forces. The specific recommendations for repair technologies developed for this project primarily address the type of damage normally encountered in concrete and masonry wall buildings; however, the policy framework developed in this document applies to buildings in general without regard to structural system.

The guidance on policies and techniques for repair of earthquake damage in this document addresses:

1. The parameters normally considered in decisions on the scope of repair or upgrading for buildings damaged by earthquakes

2. The formulation of these parameters in terms of the anticipated seismic performance of buildings in their pre-event, restored, and upgraded conditions

3. The process of evaluating anticipated seismic performance to decide whether to accept, restore, or upgrade earthquake-damaged buildings

4. The development of repair strategies to meet performance goals

5. Specific repair techniques to address damaged structural components in concrete and masonry wall buildings

1.3 Basis

The policy framework and repair techniques in this document are based on the evaluation of the effects of earthquake damage on the anticipated future performance of buildings. *FEMA 306: The Evaluation of Earthquake-Damaged Concrete and Masonry Wall Buildings — Basic Procedures Manual* (ATC, 1998a) documents the performance-based evaluation procedures. The procedures and criteria in FEMA 306 address:

1. The investigation and documentation of damage caused by earthquakes

2. The classification of the damage for building components according to mode of structural behavior and severity

3. The evaluation of the effects of the damage on the performance of the building during future earthquakes

4. The development of hypothetical measures that would restore the performance to that of the undamaged building

FEMA 307: The Evaluation of Earthquake-Damaged Concrete and Masonry Wall Buildings — Technical Resources (ATC, 1998b) provides supplemental data that facilitates use of the FEMA 306 procedures. The evaluation procedures build, to the extent possible, on existing performance-based procedures in the FEMA 273 and FEMA 274 reports, *NEHRP Guidelines for the Seismic Rehabilitation of Buildings* (ATC, 1997a), and companion *Commentary* (ATC, 1997b) and the ATC-40 report, *Seismic Evaluation and Retrofit of Concrete Buildings* (ATC, 1996). The intention is to document and adapt the existing state of knowledge rather than to develop completely new techniques. This approach also contributes to consistency of language, nomenclature, and technical concepts among emerging procedures intended for use by structural engineers.

As a part of the research program for FEMA 306, 307 and this document (FEMA 308), two issues working groups focused on the key aspects of adapting and enhancing the existing technology to the evaluation and repair of earthquake-damaged buildings. The general scope of work for each group is outlined in FEMA 307. The scope of work for the Materials Working Group included the review and summary of repair techniques for concrete and masonry wall buildings. The group reviewed experimental and analytical research reports, technical papers, standards, manufacturers' specifications, and practical example applications relating to the repair of damage in concrete and masonry walls and infill panels. The primary interest was the repair of earthquake damage to structural components. The review focused on materials and methods of installation and tests for assessing the effectiveness of repair techniques for cracking, crushing, and deterioration of concrete or masonry; and yielding, fracture, and deterioration of reinforcing steel. Based on the review, practical guidelines for damage repair were developed and are contained in this document (FEMA 308). These guidelines consist of outline specifications for equipment, materials, and procedures required to execute the repairs as well as criteria for quality control and verification of field installations. The efficacy and advisability of various techniques are discussed in relation to the objective of restoring and supplementing the force-deformation behavior of individual components.

1.4 Document Overview

This document comprises three major parts. First, background material on repair of earthquake-damaged buildings is summarized in Chapter 2. This consists of some discussion of experiences of communities after recent past earthquakes. The result is the identification of some common issues and parameters for earthquake repair policies and procedures, as well as some technical impediments to the overall process.

Chapter 3 briefly reviews the performance-based damage evaluation procedures of FEMA 306. It also introduces a policy framework based on building performance parameters. Recommendations are offered to both public policy agencies and private-sector building owners to facilitate the use of the performance-based framework.

Finally, Chapter 4 discusses the implementation of repairs. Although conventional prescriptive approaches are acceptable alternatives in many simple cases, the use of performance-based standards is recommended for general application. Typical repairs are categorized according to their intended objective. Outline specifications for repairs typically applied to concrete and masonry wall buildings are tabulated.

1.5 Limitations

The policy framework for repair presented in this document incorporates parameters related to the performance characteristics of individual buildings, the shaking severity of the damaging event, performance objectives for future events, thresholds for restoration and upgrading, and others. Policy decisions include the selection of specific limits or values for some of these parameters. This document is not intended to recommend policy for the repair or upgrading of buildings beyond the use of the generic framework. Specific limits or values for controlling parameters are not recommended in this document. In some cases, examples are used for illustration. These should not be construed by the user as policy recommendations.

Earthquakes can cause damage to both the structural and the nonstructural components of buildings. This document addresses structural damage. The direct evaluation of nonstructural damage is not included. The effects of structural damage on potential future nonstructural damage can be addressed indirectly by the selection of appropriate seismic performance objectives for the evaluation procedure.

The term *damage*, when used in this document, refers to the damage suffered during the damaging earthquake by the building in its existing condition immediately before the earthquake. It is important to note that prior effects of environmental deterioration, service conditions, and previous earthquakes are considered to be pre-existing conditions and not part of the damage to be evaluated.

The procedures and criteria for evaluating and repairing damage in this document have been based on the current state of the knowledge on nonlinear inelastic behavior of structures and structural components. This knowledge will expand over time. The evaluation procedures and the information on component behavior must be adapted appropriately to reflect new information as it becomes available.

The interpretation of damage as it relates to the performance of buildings subject to earthquakes is complex and requires experience and judgment. These procedures and criteria provide a framework for an engineer to apply experience and to formulate judgments on the effects of earthquake damage on future performance. The validity of the results primarily depend on the capability of the engineer, or engineers, as opposed to the procedures and criteria themselves.

In the past, other methodologies have been used to evaluate buildings damaged in earthquakes and to design repairs. If the procedures and criteria of this document are applied retroactively to such buildings, the results may be different. Any difference is not necessarily a reflection on the competence of the individual or firm responsible for the original work. This should be judged on the basis of the procedures and criteria that were available at the time of the work.

2. Background

2.1 Introduction

The effort to improve policy regarding the repair of earthquake-damaged buildings benefits from observations on the recovery of communities after past earthquakes. Recent experience in California and Japan reflect recent recovery efforts in urban and suburban settings and a range of local damage intensities. These observations lead to a synthesis of key policy considerations. They also reveal major technical challenges that must be met before policy can be improved.

2.2 Experience in Recent Past Earthquakes

In 1975, an earthquake in northern California severely affected the small town of Oroville. Many buildings in its downtown central business district were closed due to damage. The situation also raised concern for the safety of other buildings, particularly unreinforced masonry (URM) buildings. With the assistance of several engineers, the city council quickly passed an ordinance allowing the reopening of buildings provided that repairs designed by a civil or structural engineer reduced risk to an acceptable level (Olson and Olson, 1992). These repairs did not need to comply with current code requirements. The city also began to develop criteria for evaluation and retrofit of all buildings for seismic safety. Significant opposition from the local business community soon materialized, however, because of economic concerns over the costs of repairs and mitigative actions. After a period of intense political wrangling, the city council significantly weakened the repair ordinance and defeated the proposal for evaluation and retrofit.

After the Loma Prieta earthquake of 1989, the city of San Francisco relied primarily on the San Francisco Building Code (City and County of San Francisco, 1989) as a standard for repair and upgrading of damaged buildings. The San Francisco code is based on the *Uniform Building Code* (UBC), which is prepared by the International Conference of Building Officials (ICBO). The UBC allows repairs or alterations to existing structures so long as the repairs themselves conform to the provisions of the code. Absent a change in occupancy or other major change for the building, there is no UBC requirement to upgrade the entire building to the current provisions of the UBC. San Francisco modified this section of the code to require that the building be upgraded to full compliance (at the 75% force level) when the repairs reach a certain threshold. The existing trigger in the San Francisco code at the time of Loma Prieta required full compliance (at the 75% force level) when 30% of the structure was affected by the work. In practice, this provision has been extremely difficult to interpret and apply (Holmes, 1994).

Other cities implemented requirements for seismic upgrading based on a loss of lateral-load-carrying capacity as a result of the damaging earthquake. In Oakland, California, buildings damaged by the 1989 Loma Prieta earthquake were required to be upgraded to full compliance with the UBC if they lost a certain percentage of their capacity. Buildings were divided into two risk categories, relatively high and normal. Those determined to have a high risk, based on type of construction, size, and occupancy were required to be brought into full compliance if they had lost more than 10% of their lateral-load-resisting capacity. Those in the lower-risk group could lose 20% before full upgrade was required. Exceptions to full compliance could be issued by the building official for buildings of historical significance and for those where the cost was considered economically unfeasible. Nonetheless, these exceptions still were required to conform to the 1973 UBC and the California State Historic Building Code, where applicable.

The town of Los Gatos, a small community located relatively near the epicenter of the 1989 Loma Prieta earthquake, suffered extensive damage, particularly to its historic area. Rather than adopt standards that would be applied to all types of buildings and observed damaged conditions, Los Gatos developed policies based on five categories of damaged buildings. These included historic buildings, unreinforced masonry buildings, older wood-frame dwellings, older commercial buildings of various types, and damaged masonry chimneys (Russell, 1994). The URM buildings were required to be brought into compliance with a standard essentially equivalent to Division 88 of the Los Angeles Building Code (City of Los Angeles, 1985). This is a prescriptive model building ordinance directed at risk reduction performance for unreinforced masonry buildings. Damaged buildings other than the URM structures were required to have repairs designed to meet 75% of the lateral-force requirements of the 1985 edition of the UBC. This was the current code in effect in Los Gatos at the time of the earthquake. Further, the owner's engineer was allowed to prescribe repair or strengthening only for those structural elements found to have suffered damage. In effect, this policy was consistent with the requirements for alterations and repairs in the *Uniform Building Code*.

The city of Santa Cruz, located very close to the epicenter of the 1989 Loma Prieta earthquake, also suffered severe damage to its downtown area. The city passed an ordinance requiring all damaged buildings to meet the lateral-force requirements of the 1970 UBC.

Santa Clara County near San Jose allowed damaged URM buildings to be repaired by upgrading to the requirements of their URM ordinance, which was passed immediately after the 1989 Loma Prieta Earthquake. Their requirements are similar to Division 88 in Los Angeles.

Damage caused by the Northridge earthquake in 1994 in southern California was greater overall and more widespread than damage caused by the Loma Prieta earthquake. Repair requirements varied by local jurisdiction (CSSC, 1994). In the City of Los Angeles, when the damage at a floor resulted in less than a ten percent loss of capacity along any single line of resistance, the damaged sections could be replaced with the same construction. If the damage in any single line of resistance exceeded 10% of capacity, all components in the line were required to be brought into full code compliance. If the total loss of capacity at any floor exceeded 50%, the entire lateral-force-resisting system of the entire floor had to be brought into full compliance. Because of the technical difficulty in interpreting these requirements, the recommendations of individual engineers were accepted in most cases.

In 1991, the Japan Building Disaster Prevention Association issued guidelines for the inspection and restoration of earthquake-damaged buildings (Sugano, 1996). These guidelines were generally used in the Kobe area following the earthquake in 1995. The options for dealing with damaged buildings in these guidelines include acceptance of the building in its damaged condition, repair to its pre-event condition, strengthening to a level greater than its pre-event condition, or demolition. The recommended action depends on two factors. The first is the level of damage that was sustained during the damaging event. There are five classifications for the degree of damage ranging

from "slight" to "collapse". Procedures are provided to categorize the degree of damage based on the damage observed in the field. The second factor determining the degree of repair or upgrade required for the building is the intensity of shaking in the vicinity of the building. This is designated in accordance with the Japanese Meteorological Agency intensity scale, which has five levels of shaking intensity. This scale is qualitative and similar to the Modified Mercalli Intensity scale used in the United States. These guidelines recognize that the level of repair or upgrade depends both on the amount of damage and on the intensity of shaking to which the building was subjected. It differs from the approach of the City of Oakland and others who established a loss-of-capacity criterion that apparently applies regardless of the intensity of shaking.

2.3 Basic Policy Considerations

All communities in past earthquakes addressed the challenge of recovery and reconstruction their own ways. In spite of this, observations on these experiences lead to several general conclusions and key considerations for future policy:

1. The economic impact of earthquakes is a major factor in the implementation of policies for repair and upgrading after an event. A damaging earthquake presents particularly difficult and complex problems for individual building owners and the general community. Owners may be confronted with large repair costs along with a business downturn, both caused by the earthquake. It is in the community's long-term interest to require restoration or upgrading of damaged buildings to avoid similar or greater losses in future earthquakes. In the short term, however, restrictive policies for repair can restrain vital economic recovery. Effective policy to deal with this situation is a balance of often-competing imperatives including, for example, public safety, private property rights, historic preservation, urban planning, economic development, and ethical and legal considerations.

2. There is a virtually complete lack of standards directed toward the postearthquake repair of damaged buildings. Most jurisdictions rely upon some adaptation of an existing code or model building ordinance for these guidelines. These adaptations are developed after the event in a reactive manner by city governments and engineers.

3. The policies for specific buildings are related to their occupancy and function. It seems reasonable to hold important buildings to a somewhat higher standard than others. The risk of failure associated with damage in a hospital is greater than that for single-family residences.

4. The vulnerability associated with different building types is a factor. Older buildings or those with structural systems known to pose greater risks during earthquakes (e.g., URM) are often held to more stringent requirements.

5. Insurance companies and agencies tend to measure losses by comparing the damaged condition of buildings to their pre-event condition. While this policy limits the liability of the insurer, it does little to reduce future losses, particularly for larger events.

6. There is a tolerance for some amount of damage during an earthquake. This seems logically to be related to the intensity of shaking of the damaging earthquake. If a building suffers a small amount of damage in a small or moderate event, most communities are willing to accept this damage, or, at the most, require that the building be brought back to its previous condition. On the other hand, when buildings suffer a large amount of damage in a small or moderate event, the tolerance for acceptance of the restoration to the previous condition is less. This attitude is related to the economic considerations discussed above.

2.4   Technical Impediments

Experience from recent past earthquakes demonstrates that technical improvement in engineering standards for the evaluation and repair of buildings would enhance and facilitate the recovery. Holmes (1994) summarized the primary impediments to effective standards for the evaluation and repair of earthquake damage. These are consolidated and summarized as follows:

1. *Lack of formalized methods for analyzing the realistic effects of earthquake shaking and resulting damage on the performance of buildings and their components.* Traditionally, the focus of structural analysis and design has been on forces. This is due to the fact that the most obvious structural demand that most buildings face are their own weight and the imposed vertical load. These are easily and

acceptably treated as static forces. Over the years, it has become increasingly clear that the dynamic loads imparted to buildings by earthquakes are fundamentally different from static loads. The magnitude of the demand depends on the weight and stiffness of the building. Inevitably, the structure yields to dissipate energy during an earthquake. When it does, ductility, the ability to deform inelastically without abrupt loss of strength, is a critical capacity parameter. Stiffness, energy dissipation, and ductility are all dependent on displacements, as is damage.

Traditional analyses of forces assume linearly-elastic structural response. Therefore, the global demand is reduced and the allowable component force capacities are increased to account indirectly for inelastic behavior. The actual global displacement of the structure and the distortion of its components remain obscure, at best. Since damage depends on the actual displacements, the condition of the structure for a specific level of force is very difficult to characterize. This can be visualized by examining a typical inelastic capacity curve for a building (see Figure 2-1). As the structure begins to yield, the curve generally flattens with respect to the displacement axis. In the inelastic region, a small change in force can result in a large change in displacement. This is a fundamental improvement in analysis that is currently emerging in engineering practice (ATC, 1996; 1997a,b).

The key to realistic evaluation of the effects of earthquake damage on performance is a methodology that focuses on displacements rather than forces.

2. *Limited information on the behavior of structural components particularly on the effectiveness of repairs, the relationship between repair techniques and damage intensity, and the effects of local repair on global behavior.* Traditional codes and structural analysis techniques address structural component behavior in the linear range. Little data on inelastic behavior have been formally compiled from available research and test results. Observations of damage (e.g., crack size and extent) to components have not been related to changes in structural properties. There are few standards for design and construction related to the repairs normally used for damaged structural components, nor are there readily avail-

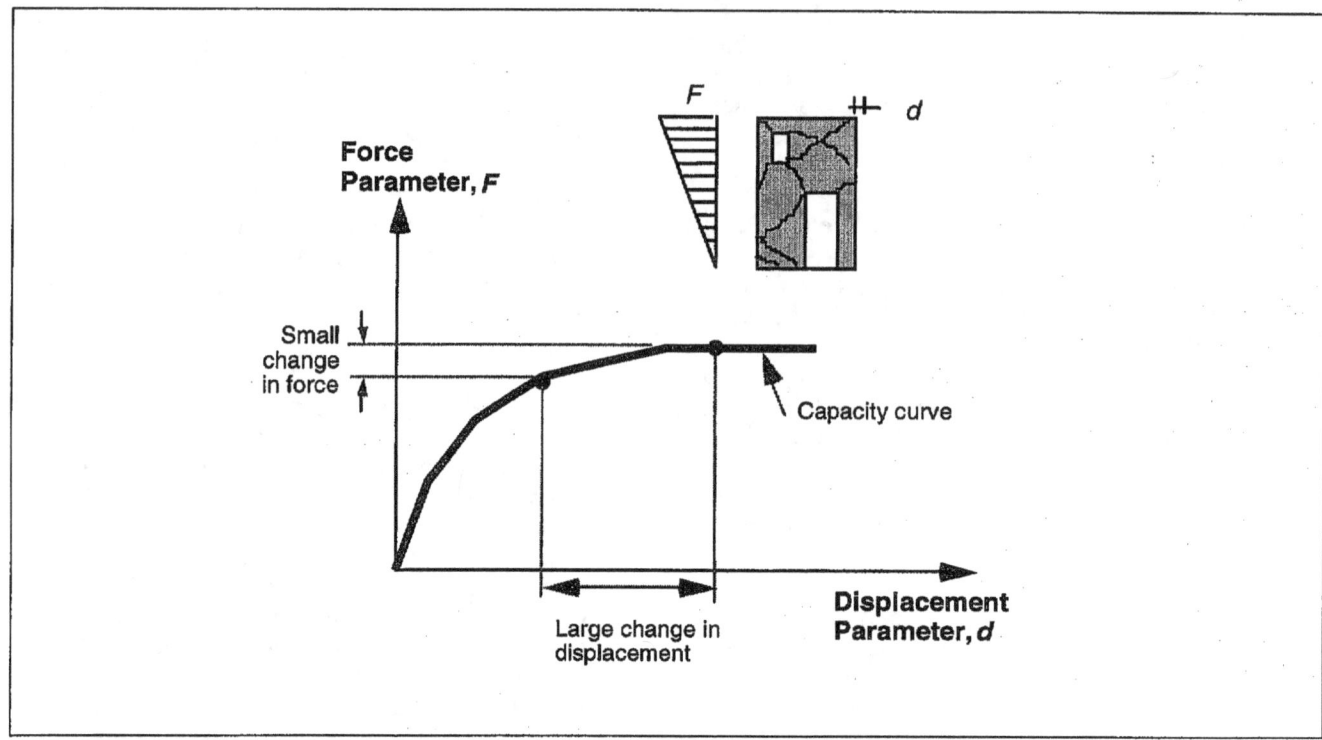

Figure 2-1 *Sensitivity of displacement to changes in force*

able data on the effect of repairs on structural properties.

The state of knowledge on component behavior needs to be documented and augmented as necessary to relate damage (and repair) to structural performance.

3. *Inadequate methods of measuring the significance of damage with respect to future risks.* When considering what to do with a building damaged by an earthquake, a logical question is: "How does the damage affect what will happen in a future earthquake?" Design codes and conventional engineering methodologies are prescriptive, and they do not provide specific insight into seismic performance of new or damaged existing buildings. The costs to upgrade a damaged building to current code provisions are rarely trivial. The implication of a community building department requirement for such upgrade work is that the future consequences of earthquakes to the community are worth the price. Similarly, the decision by a building owner to accept a damaged building without repair is tacit acceptance of the future costs.

Effective earthquake repair policy and individual decisions require better estimates of future seismic performance.

3. Performance-Based Policy Framework

3.1 Introduction

In practice, successful recovery after a damaging earthquake depends on effective policies and a cooperative effort between the private and public sectors. The action to be taken on a damaged building is ultimately the responsibility of the owner. Normally, however, the owner's options are constrained through building regulations intended to protect public safety and to reduce future economic losses. The experience in past earthquakes outlined in Chapter 2 suggests that policy planning for recovery in advance of earthquakes might greatly improve the process. Such planning could address key considerations encountered after past earthquakes. The performance-based procedures for the evaluation of earthquake-damaged buildings presented in FEMA 306 and FEMA 307 can provide improved technical information to facilitate both the planning and recovery efforts. These procedures allow policies and decisions to be fundamentally based on estimates of the performance of damaged, restored, or upgraded buildings.

3.2 Basic Alternatives

There are a number of alternatives for dealing with a building that has been damaged by an earthquake. For the purposes of developing a policy framework to facilitate the decision-making process, three alternatives are considered:

- *Accept* the building for continued use in its damaged condition. Sometimes the damage is obviously slight, implying that the building is only marginally worse off than before the damaging earthquake. If the damage is greater and the building seems more prone to future damage, perhaps the occupancy can be changed to reduce the risk and, at the same time, avoid repairs.

- *Restore* the building to its pre-event condition. It seems logical to fix the damage that was done. In fact, this is the traditional approach in the insurance industry. The restored building would behave in future earthquakes as it would have in its pre-event condition. The risks would be no greater than before the damaging event.

- *Upgrade* the building to a condition of improved seismic performance compared to its pre-event

condition. Earthquake damage can reveal significant deficiencies in buildings. The risks associated with the building in future earthquakes, even in a restored condition, might be too large. In this case, the repairs are designed to improve the future performance and to reduce risks.

Selecting among these basic alternatives for a damaged building requires consideration of all of the policy issues outlined in Chapter 2. The decision process and the alternatives themselves imply a capability to answer a fundamental technical question: How can the acceptability of a building's anticipated earthquake performance be measured? A benchmark is needed to compare the performance of the building in damaged, restored, and upgraded states.

3.3 Damage Evaluation Procedure

There has been a tendency to attempt to gauge the effect of earthquake damage by estimating the loss of lateral-force-resisting capacity of the structure (Hanson, 1996). It has been assumed that this loss can be related to the observed width and extent of concrete and masonry cracks in damaged shear-wall buildings, for example. In reality, there is widespread disagreement on the effect of cracking on capacity and skepticism on the suitability of force capacity itself as a parameter for measuring damage.

Recent progress in the development of performance-based evaluation techniques allows a more meaningful measurement of the effect of damage on concrete and masonry wall buildings (FEMA 273/274, and ATC-40). Performance-based procedures characterize the effects of earthquake shaking on structures in terms of displacement limit states. The adaptation of these procedures to the evaluation of earthquake-damaged buildings is presented in FEMA 306. The evaluation procedure assumes that when an earthquake causes damage to a building, a competent engineer can assess the effects, at least partially, through visual inspection augmented by investigative tests, structural analysis, and knowledge of the building construction. By determining how the structural damage has changed structural properties, it is possible to compare analytically the future performance of the damaged building with that of the building in its undamaged condition. It is also feasible to investigate the effectiveness of potential measures to restore or upgrade the damaged building.

3.3.1 Performance Objectives

The proposed evaluation procedure is performance-based; that is, it measures acceptability (and changes in acceptability caused by previous damage) on the basis of the degree to which the structure achieves one or more performance levels for the hazard posed by one or more hypothetical future earthquakes. A performance level typically is defined by a particular damage state for a building. Commonly-used performance levels, in order of decreasing amounts of damage, are collapse prevention, life safety, and immediate occupancy. Hazards associated with future hypothetical earthquakes commonly are defined in terms of ground shaking amplitudes with a certain likelihood of being exceeded over a defined time period, or in terms of a characteristic earthquake likely to occur on a given fault. The combination of a performance level and a hazard defines a performance objective (ATC, 1996; 1997a, b).

3.3.2 Global Displacement Parameters

The performance-based procedures use structural analysis methods that focus on realistic estimates of the displacements of a building subjected to seismic ground motions. These nonlinear static procedures (NSPs) generate a plot, called a capacity curve (see Figure 3-1), that relates a global displacement parameter (at the roof level, for example) to the lateral force imposed on the structure. There are several available NSPs, and they differ from one another in the technique used to estimate the maximum global displacement, d_d, for a given ground motion. The damage evaluation procedure provided in FEMA 306 uses NSPs to compare a global displacement capacity limit for a specific performance level, d_c (Figure 3-2), with a maximum global displacement demand for a particular ground shaking hazard, d_d (Figure 3-3). The ratio of the displacement capacity, d_c, of the building for the specific performance level to the displacement demand, d_d, for a specific hazard is a measure of the degree to which the building meets the associated performance objective.

3.3.3 Structural Components

The FEMA 306 evaluation method uses a model of the building composed of its structural components. The

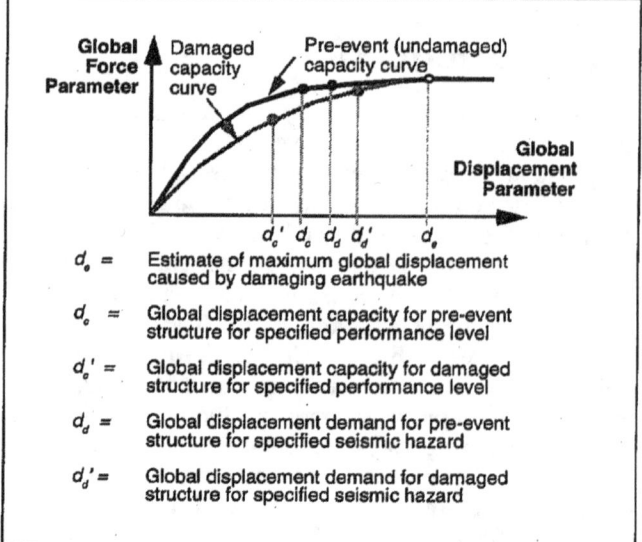

d_e = Estimate of maximum global displacement caused by damaging earthquake

d_c = Global displacement capacity for pre-event structure for specified performance level

d_c' = Global displacement capacity for damaged structure for specified performance level

d_d = Global displacement demand for pre-event structure for specified seismic hazard

d_d' = Global displacement demand for damaged structure for specified seismic hazard

Figure 3-1   *Capacity curves from nonlinear static procedures.*

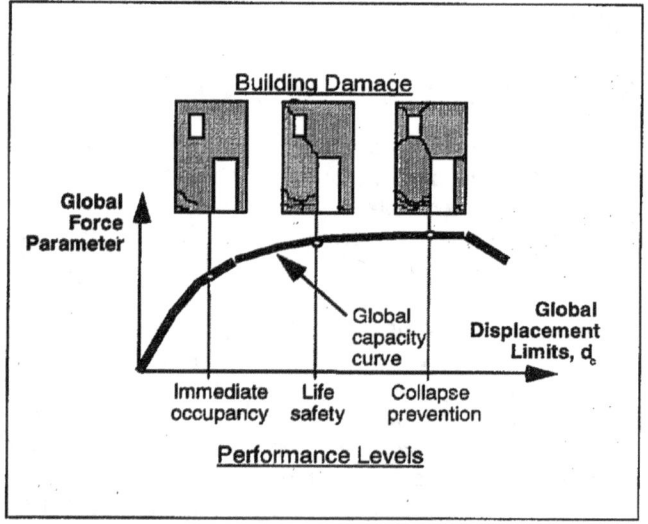

Figure 3-2   *Global displacement capacities, d_c, for various performance levels*

behavior of the structure in its undamaged, damaged, and restored conditions is controlled by associated inelastic force-deformation relationships for each component. The model for analysis of the building comprises an assembly of individual structural components. The force-deformation characteristics for individual components are idealizations of representative hysteretic behavior under cyclic loading

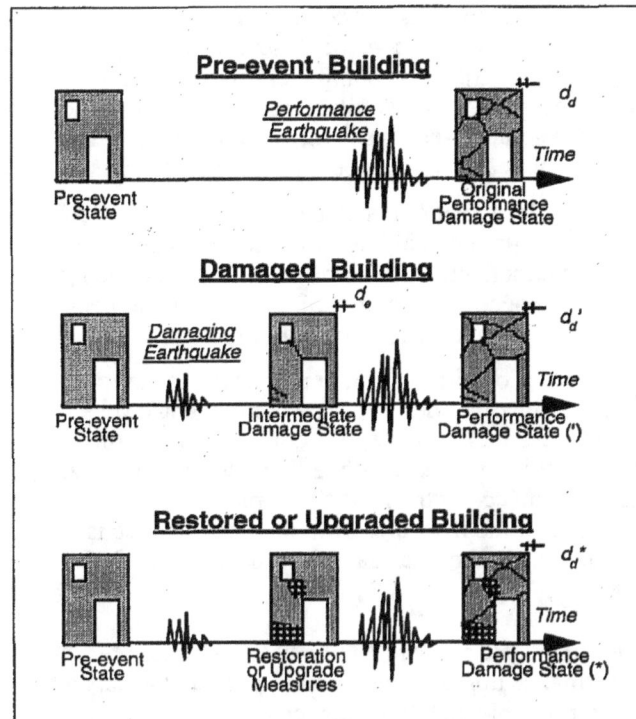

Figure 3-3 *Global displacement demand for undamaged, damaged, and restored/ upgraded conditions*

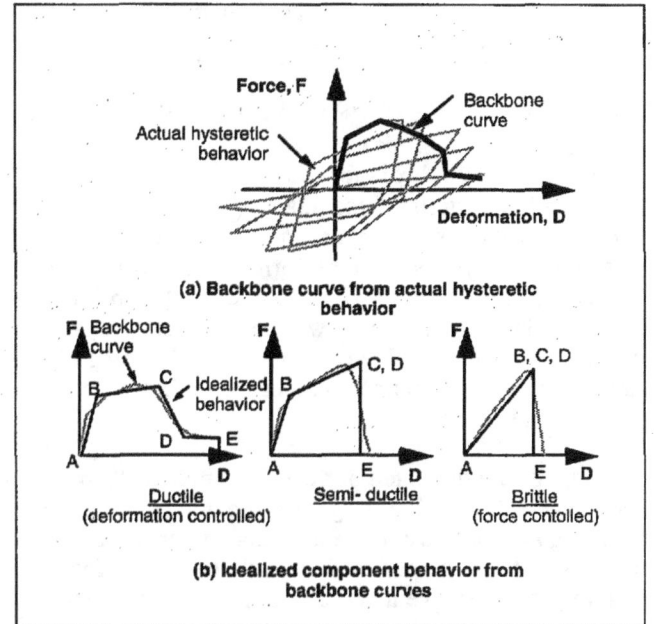

Figure 3-4 *Structural component force-deformation characteristics*

conditions (Figure 3-4). For a given global displacement of a structure subjected to a given lateral load pattern, there is an associated deformation for each of the structural components of the building. Since inelastic deformation indicates component damage, then the maximum global displacement, d_d, to occur during an earthquake represents a structural damage state for the building in terms of inelastic deformations for each of its components. The capacity of a given structure for a given performance level is represented by the maximum global displacement, d_c, at which the damage is on the verge of exceeding the limit for the specific performance level. For example, the collapse-prevention capacity of a building might be the roof displacement at which the associated damage would result in one or more of the column components being in danger of imminent collapse.

At the beginning of the evaluation process, the engineer identifies basic components and documents the damage to each. The global displacement parameters for the

building are calculated using component properties for the pre-event conditions (d_c and d_d). The structural properties of the components then are modified to reflect the effects of the observed damage using factors contained in FEMA 306 supplemented by additional information contained in FEMA 307. This allows the evaluation of the global displacement parameters for the building in its damaged condition (d'_c and d'_d). Information also is provided to modify component properties to reflect the effects of repairs to restore or upgrade on global displacement parameters (d^*_c and d^*_d) for the building.

3.4 Performance Capacity and Loss

The ratios of global displacement limits or capacities (d_c, d'_c, d^*_c) for a specific performance level to the corresponding displacement demands (d_d, d'_d, d^*_d) for a specific seismic hazard define indices of measurement (P, P', P^*) of the ability of an undamaged ( ), damaged ('), or restored or upgraded (*) building to meet a specific performance objective (see Figure 3-1). These indices are:

$P = d_c / d_d$ Pre-event performance index,

$P' = d_c' / d_d'$ Damaged performance index,

$P^* = d_c^* / d_d^*$ Restored or upgraded performance index.

If a performance index is less than one, the implication is that the building in its undamaged ( ), damaged ('), or repaired (*) state is not able to meet the specific performance objective. If a performance index is 1.0 or greater, the implication is that it can meet the objective. Note that these indices are always associated with a specific performance objective. The same building may have different performance indices for different performance objectives.

The ratio of the damaged performance index, P', to the undamaged, P, for a building for a specific performance objective is a measure of the anticipated performance capacity of the damaged building relative to that for the building in its pre-event state. The loss in performance capacity caused by damaging ground motion is:

$$L = 1 - (P'/P)$$

3.5 Restoration or Upgrade Procedure

The procedures of FEMA 306 include guidelines for formulating repair measures to restore the damaged building to its pre-event performance capability. If the performance capability of the structure for a selected performance objective is diminished by the effects of earthquake damage ($P' < P$) the magnitude of the economic loss is quantified by the costs of performance restoration measures. These are hypothetical actions that, if implemented, would result in future performance approximately equivalent to that of the undamaged building ($P^* \approx P$). Performance restoration measures may take several different forms:

a. Component restoration entails the repair of individual components to restore structural properties that were diminished as a result of the earthquake damage. For example, cracks in a shear wall might be injected with grout to restore component strength and stiffness. Outline specifications for typical repairs for concrete and masonry wall buildings are included in this document in Chapter 4.

b. An extreme case of component repair is complete replacement. A severely damage wall section might be completely removed and replaced with a similar or improved component. In some cases, this is the only alternative. In other cases, it may be an economic alternative.

c. Performance can also be restored by the addition of supplemental lateral-resisting elements or components. Instead of repairing or replacing a damaged section of wall, a new wall element might be installed in another location.

The process of formulating performance restoration measures involves developing a component-level strategy that includes one, or a combination, of the three alternatives. The measures are then tested by analyzing the performance of the modified structure and adjusting the scope of the measures until the performance is approximately the same as that of the pre-event building ($P^* \approx P$).

The same basic strategy can be used to formulate performance upgrade measures to provide the capacity to meet the selected performance objective ($P^* \approx 1.0$).

3.6 Relative Seismic Demand

Decisions regarding an appropriate policy for the acceptance, restoration, or upgrade of earthquake-damaged buildings, depend in part on the severity of the damaging event (Section 3.8). The severity of shaking is a function of the magnitude of the damaging event as well as the epicentral distance and the amplification caused by site soils. The Modified Mercalli Intensity scale or other intensity scales can be useful in formulating a qualitative perspective of shaking severity for a specific building relative to others in the vicinity. Quantitative parameters include site peak ground acceleration and spectral acceleration at the period of the building.

Displacement-based analysis procedures also can be used to gauge the relative severity of ground motion demand on specific buildings. FEMA 306 provides guidance on estimating the maximum displacement, d_e, caused by the damaging ground motion using the capacity curve and the damage observations for a specific building. The capacity curve can also be used to estimate the maximum displacement demand, d_d, for a performance ground motion. The ratio, S, of the real global displacement, d_e, caused by the damaging ground motion to the hypothetical displacement demand, d_d, for the performance ground motion is an index of relative displacement demand and is represented as:

$$S = d_e / d_d$$

The relative displacement demand provides an improved and unambiguous measure of the demand on the building associated with the damaging earthquake for several reasons. First, it is a measure that applies directly to the specific building and site. Secondly, the basis of measurement, displacement, is a better index of damage for buildings than acceleration. Finally, the index is normalized relative to a defined performance objective.

3.7 Relative Risk

The capacity curve for a pre-event ( ), damaged ('), or repaired (*) building allows one to estimate

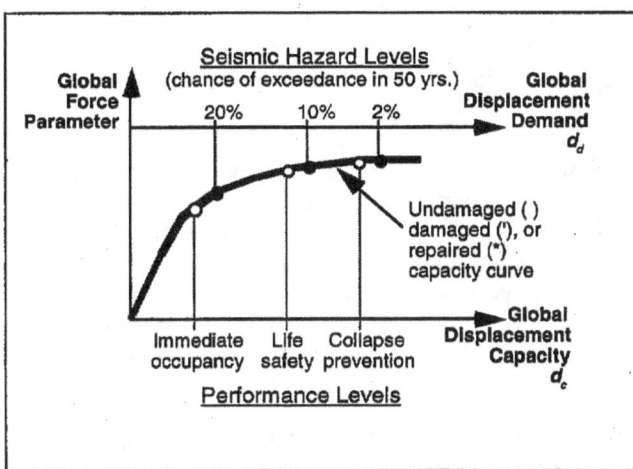

Figure 3-5 *Global displacement demands and capacities*

displacement demands for various levels of seismic hazard as shown in Figure 3-5. These may be generated using nonlinear static procedures according to the recommendations in FEMA 306, in conjunction with the appropriate capacity curve. In Figure 3-5 these are plotted on the upper horizontal axis noting their chance of exceedance in 50 years. Component acceptability criteria in conjunction with capacity curves also can be

used to define global displacement limits for various performance levels (e.g., immediate occupancy, life safety, collapse prevention). These are shown in Figure 3-5 along the lower horizontal axis. The combined plot provides a complete picture of the risks associated with the particular repair alternative.

Global displacement demand for various repair alternatives can also be plotted versus a risk parameter as shown in Figure 3-6. The intersection of a global displacement capacity value, for a selected performance level, with the corresponding displacement demand curve allows an estimate of the risk that the performance level would be exceeded for a given repair alternative. Doing this for several repair alternatives, as

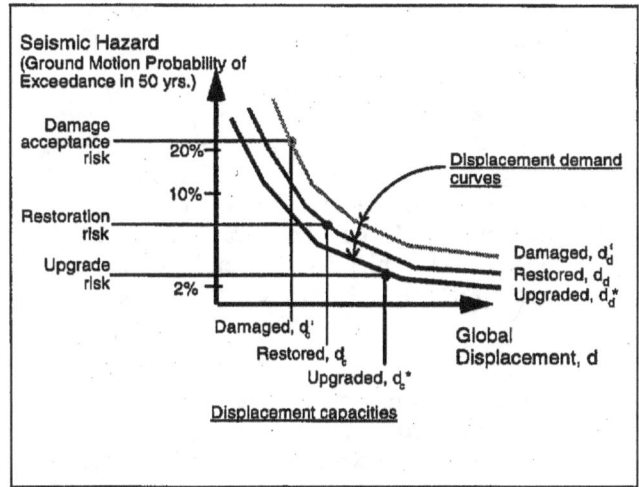

Figure 3-6 *Risk associated with damage acceptance, restoration, and upgrade for a specific performance objective*

shown in Figure 3-6, provides a comparison of the risks associated with each alternative for the selected performance level. For example, suppose that the performance level of interest is life safety. Figure 3-6 illustrates that the chance that the global displacement demand would exceed the life safety capacity of the damaged structure is slightly higher than 20% in fifty years. Restoration of the structure to its pre-event condition would reduce the life safety risk to less than 10%. The upgrade could reduce risk to just above 2% or approximately ten times less than the damaged structure in this illustration.

3.8 Thresholds for Restoration and Upgrade

The decision on an appropriate course of action (accept damage, restore, or upgrade) for a specific building damaged during an earthquake depends on a number of interrelated factors discussed below:

a. *Relative Severity of Damaging Ground Motion.* The tolerance for damage caused by relatively large earthquake ground motions is logically greater than if the same damage were caused by small ground motions. It makes sense that a building significantly damaged by small ground motions is a good candidate for upgrading. After earthquake ground motions at about the design level for which damage is expected, a less restrictive policy on upgrading will facilitate the economic recovery of the community.

b. *The acceptability of performance characteristics of the building after the damaging earthquake.* If the damaged building is capable of meeting reasonable performance objectives in its damaged state, repair or upgrading may be unnecessary. It is also possible that short-term performance objectives, lower than those appropriate for the longer term, may be reasonable to use in some circumstances, eliminating the need for immediate action.

c. *The acceptability of performance characteristics of the building before the damaging earthquake.* The decision between restoration and upgrading is largely controlled by the acceptability of the restored performance, which would be equivalent to that before the earthquake. It is not logical to restore a building to a poor level of expected performance.

d. *The change in performance characteristics of the building caused by the damaging earthquake.* If the damaging earthquake causes a large decrease in the performance characteristics of a building, restoration or upgrading are obviously more advisable than if the loss were small. Small losses, particularly for large earthquakes, are often acceptable.

e. *Nonseismic issues related to the condition and use of the building.* Nonseismic deficiencies (e.g., disabled access, fire and life safety, programmatic, maintenance) are important considerations. So is the anticipated future use of a building and any change in appropriate seismic performance objectives. It makes little sense to extend the life of a building significantly without addressing seismic deficiencies.

Some of these factors governing decisions on acceptance, restoration, or upgrading have no fundamental technical basis. The rationale for allowing some leeway in these decisions to account for nontechnical considerations is based on the precedent established in past earthquakes and common sense. It is helpful, however, to establish quantifiable parameters to represent the results of judgement and experience.

The performance indices for the building in its pre-event (P) and damaged (P') condition can be determined using the relative performance analysis procedures of FEMA 306. Component acceptability and global displacement demand control the thresholds for restoration and repair because the performance index for both the pre-event structure (P) and the damaged structure (P') are defined as the ratio of global displacement capacity (d_c or d_c') to the global displacement demand (d_d or d_d'). The behavior of individual components, as discussed in Section 3.3.3 and FEMA 306, governs global displacement capacities. Performance loss, L, is a function of the performance indices.

Boundaries between acceptance and restoration, and between acceptance or restoration and upgrading can be defined as in Tables 3-1 and 3-2. The parameters introduced in these tables can be plotted, for a given damaging earthquake with relative displacement demand, S, as illustrated in Figure 3-7a and b and used as a guide for the need for restoration or upgrading of a damaged building.

The performance loss (L) for the selected objective is determined and plotted as a horizontal line as in Figure 3-7a and b. Figure 3-7a illustrates the boundary between restoration or upgrade and acceptance of the damage. Figure 3-7b illustrates the boundary between damage acceptance (or restoration) and upgrade. Turning first to Figure 3-7a, the point (P', L) is used to determine if the damage can be accepted. If the damaged building is capable of meeting reasonable performance objectives, repair or upgrading is unnecessary. The restoration boundary between acceptance of the damage and the need for restoration or upgrade is defined by the parameters in Table 3-1. If the performance loss (L) is small, then restoration or

Table 3-1	Parameters governing whether damage is acceptable (see Figure 3-7a)
$L_{r(min)}$ =	Performance loss threshold below which restoration is not required regardless of the Damaged Performance Index, P'. (Avoids requiring restoration when the effects of damage on performance are small. This threshold would be comparatively lower for damaging earthquakes with small relative displacement demand (S) and higher for large ones.)
P'_{min} =	Damaged Performance Index limit below which restoration is required unless the Performance Loss is less than $L_{r(min)}$. (Limits how far the Damaged Performance Index (P') can fall and still be acceptable without restoration. This limit would be comparatively lower for damaging earthquakes with large relative displacement demand (S) and higher for smaller ones.)
$L_{r(max)}$ =	Performance Loss threshold above which restoration is required unless the Damaged Performance Index exceeds P'_{max}. (Requires restoration for relatively large losses unless the Damaged Performance Index (P') is high. The threshold would be comparatively lower for damaging earthquakes with small relative displacement demand (S) and higher for larger ones.)
P'_{max} =	Damaged Performance Index limit above which restoration is not required regardless of the Performance Loss. (Establishes when the Damaged Performance Index (P') is acceptable without restoration. This limit would be comparatively lower for damaging earthquakes with large relative displacement demand (S) and higher for smaller ones.)

Table 3-2	Parameters governing whether restoration is acceptable (see Figure 3-7b)
$L_{u(min)}$ =	Performance Loss threshold below which upgrading is not required regardless of the Pre-event (Undamaged) Performance Index. (Avoids requiring upgrading when the effects of damage on performance are small. The threshold would be relatively lower for damaging earthquakes with small relative displacement demand (S) and higher for larger ones.)
P_{min} =	Pre-event Performance Index limit below which upgrading is required unless the Performance Loss is less than $L_{u(min)}$. (Establishes when the Pre-event Performance Index (P) is acceptable without upgrading. This limit would be relatively lower for damaging earthquakes with high relative displacement demand (S) and higher for smaller ones.)
$L_{u(max)}$ =	Performance Loss threshold above which upgrading is required unless the Pre-event Performance Index exceeds P_{max}. (Requires upgrading for relatively large losses unless the Pre-event Performance Index (P) is high. The threshold would be comparatively lower for damaging earthquakes with small relative displacement demand (S) and higher for larger ones.)
P_{max} =	Pre-event Performance Index limit above which upgrading is not required regardless of Performance Loss. (Establishes when the Pre-event Performance Index (P) is acceptable without upgrading. This limit would be comparatively lower for damaging earthquakes with large relative displacement demand (S) and higher for smaller ones.)

upgrading might not be required since the change in performance is negligible. This concept is represented by the horizontal line at $L_{r(min)}$. If the loss exceeds the minimum, then the decision on whether to accept the damage is controlled by how close the damaged performance index is to P'_{min} and P'_{max}. The lower end of the sloping portion of the restoration boundary represents the limit (P'_{min}). As the loss increases there is logically less tolerance for a lower damaged performance index (P'). As the loss increases further, there comes a point $L_{r(max)}$, at which the damaged

performance index must be greater than P'_{max} ($P' > P'_{max}$) if damage is to be acceptable regardless of the loss. If the damaged performance index (P', L) is within the restoration boundary, then either restoration or upgrading is required.

The parameters affecting the decision between upgrade or restoration are illustrated in Figure 3-7b. The decision between upgrade or restoration is controlled by the loss (L) and the pre-event performance index (P). The upgrade boundary is delineated similarly to the restoration boundary using the parameters in Table 3-2.

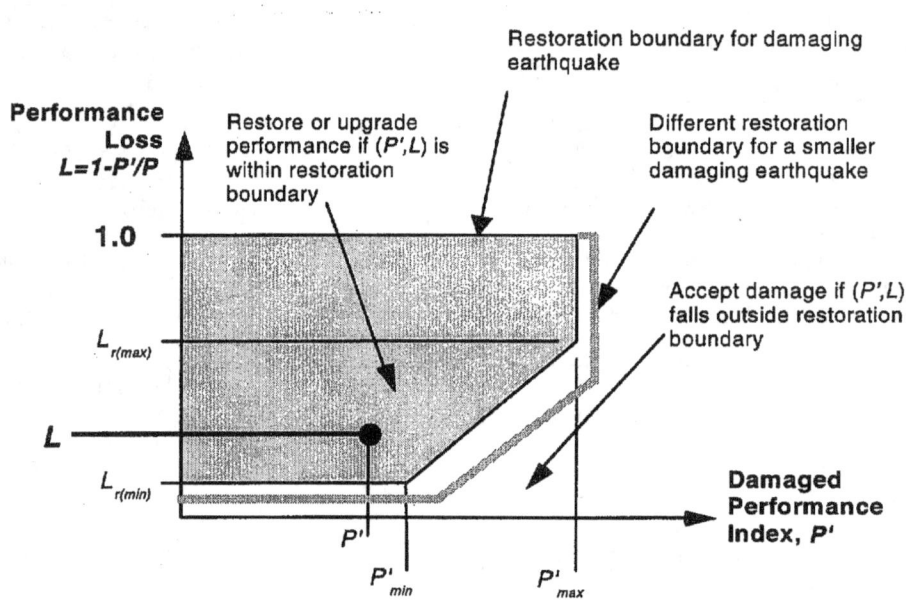

a) Relationship between acceptance of damage versus repair or upgrade

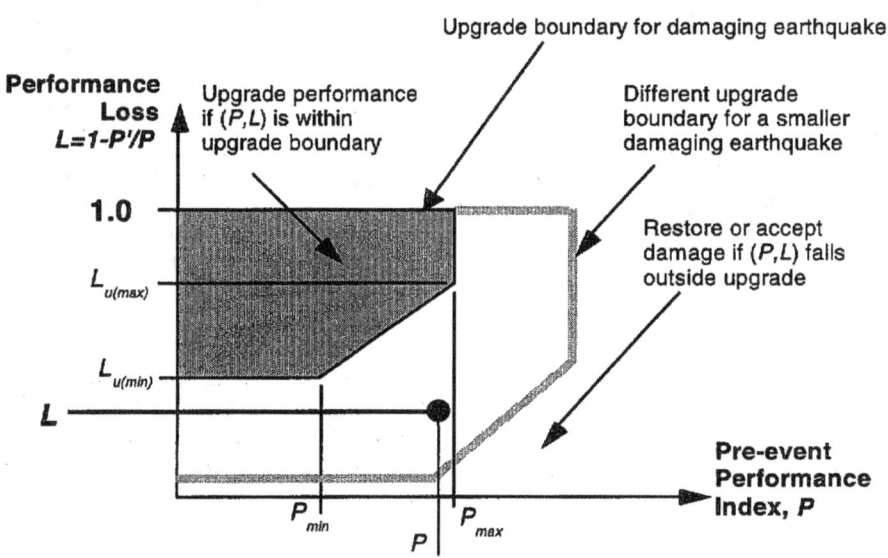

b) Relationship between acceptance of damage or restoration versus upgrade

Figure 3-7   *Thresholds and performance limits for restoration and upgrade of earthquake-damaged buildings*

It is important to recognize that the parameters affecting decisions between acceptance, restoration, and upgrade may vary with the size of the damaging earthquake as defined by the relative displacement demand, S, for a given building. This reflects the logic that greater losses and lower performance indices are tolerable for larger earthquakes. The effects of this variable on the restoration and upgrade boundaries are illustrated in Figure 3-7a and b with the lighter boundaries for smaller earthquakes. The intersection of the pre-event performance index with the loss line in Figure 3-7b falls outside the upgrade boundary indicating that restoration is sufficient. However if this same loss had occurred in the smaller earthquake, the intersection of P and L would fall within the boundary indicating that upgrade is necessary.

3.9 Policy Implications and Limitations of Component Acceptability and Displacement Demand

If component acceptability and global displacement demand criteria are applied to both the pre-event and damaged structures consistently, the effects of damage, as gauged by the scope and cost of measures to restore performance, are not sensitive to variations in the criteria. In the evaluation of the effects of damage, the numerical value of the performance indices and loss are not meaningful in themselves. The same is not the case when these parameters are used to facilitate policy decisions for acceptance, repair, or upgrade. Component acceptability and displacement demand affect these decisions directly.

The current provisions of FEMA 273 (ATC, 1997a) and ATC-40 (ATC, 1996) limit global displacements for the performance level under consideration (e.g., Immediate Occupancy, Life Safety, Collapse Prevention) to that at which any single component reaches its acceptability limit. There is not universal agreement among researchers and practitioners regarding the accuracy of these acceptability provisions for several reasons:

1. The amount of available research data on the force/ deformation characteristics of various components for different behavior modes is not sufficient. The interpretation of test data is also difficult since standard protocols have not been available.

2. The acceptability limits for deformation of individual components are difficult to generalize. Two of

the key findings of the research effort for this project are that the mode of component behavior controls acceptability and that the mode of behavior is not always what might be predicted using analysis procedures, similar to those of FEMA 273 and ATC-40, intended primarily for design. This concern is obviated to some degree by the use of FEMA 306, which requires that component force/ deformation relationships match the mode of behavior observed in the field from the effects of damage.

3. In many structures, the failure of a single component to meet acceptability criteria is not an accurate indicator of global acceptability. For example, the lack of acceptability for life safety of a highly shear-critical, vertical-load-bearing, wall pier might indeed limit global acceptability. By contrast, the unacceptability of a single coupling beam carrying only a small local gravity load in addition to earthquake forces may not alone be sufficient justification for a global life safety limit. In reality, global displacement limits are a complex function of component behavior and acceptability. Important considerations include the number and location of critical components, vertical load transfer, and interactions among components, particularly with respect to the development of collapse mechanisms.

There is also controversy with regard to the determination of maximum displacement demand for use with nonlinear static procedures. FEMA 273 emphasizes the use of the displacement coefficient method while ATC-40 documents the capacity spectrum method. In some circumstances these two alternatives can lead to different estimates of displacements.

The lack of complete consensus on component acceptability and displacement demand is understandable, since nonlinear static procedures have not been used extensively to date. They still require a great deal of engineering judgment, and common sense, to produce reliable results. Over the years acceptability limits and displacement demand are likely to become more accurate and less controversial.

Use of the performance-based framework introduced in this document requires the understanding of the controlling influence of the component acceptability and displacement demand criteria. The absolute numerical values for Performance Indices and Loss parameters have no significance in and of themselves. They are only as reliable and meaningful as the component acceptability and displacement demand criteria used to generate them. If the acceptability criteria are overly conservative or liberal, the Performance Indices will directly reflect this with a relatively low or high value. The use of the framework and associated parameters must include a definitive and consistent specification for the component acceptability and displacement demand criteria. The parameters themselves then provide a convenient way to measure performance and loss within the limitations of the specified criteria.

3.10 Public Sector Policy Planning Recommendations

Public agencies, particularly building authorities, can prepare for a future earthquake by taking action beforehand. The following are some suggestions related specifically to the procedures developed in this document:

1. Establish seismic performance objectives for buildings within the community. These can be modeled on existing standards including FEMA 273 and ATC 40. Selection of appropriate objectives should be based on the size, age, occupancy, and function of the individual building.

2. Adopt a seismic hazard demand standard. These also can be generated using FEMA 273 or ATC 40. Communities may wish to develop more detailed specific earthquake ground motion or other seismic hazard specifications based on regional or local conditions.

3. Adopt loss thresholds for repair and upgrading based on the intensity of future seismic events. Guidance on the actual value for these thresholds can only be qualitative at this point. In the future, it is possible that research on loss and economic recovery after earthquakes can shed some light on the appropriate levels of tolerable damage. Similarly, tolerable levels of performance deficiencies can be developed for damaged buildings.

4. Review and document the extent to which non-seismic compliance requirements are imposed on the repair and upgrading process. Issues for prior consideration include disabled access, fire and life safety, and historic buildings.

5. Establish programs for encouraging building owners to document the anticipated performance characteristics for their building. In some cases, mandatory investigations or retrofit may be appropriate. Even if this cannot be implemented, building owners should be allowed to investigate performance deficiencies without the requirement to address them immediately.

6. Establish a repository of public information on earthquake hazards and the vulnerabilities of buildings. Building database technologies such as those specified in HAZUS (NIBS, 1997) and ATC-36 (ATC, in preparation) can facilitate this effort. Such databases are useful both before, immediately after, and during the recovery process of an earthquake.

3.11 Private Policy Planning Recommendations

In the private sector, building owners and occupants can benefit greatly by planning an investigation before an earthquake. Some useful efforts are listed below:

1. Assemble design and construction information on the specific building or group of buildings of concern. Structural information is particularly important to the investigation of damage. This might consist of drawings, calculations, and previous reports.

2. Engage a qualified engineer to document the existing condition of each building. This entails mapping existing cracks and other damage that may be due to previous earthquakes or other causes. This information serves to establish a baseline for any future damage that may occur in an earthquake. Additionally, it gives the engineer a chance to become familiar with the basic structural characteristics of the building.

3. Evaluate the need for and implement, if necessary, further investigations to determine the component characteristics of the building in its current state. The scope of these investigations can range from rather straightforward and inexpensive to very sophisticated analyses. The knowledge about the future performance of the building is important to the building owner or occupant even if immediate upgrading or repair is not possible.

4. Consider the effects that earthquakes may have on the business enterprise carried out in the building.

This knowledge, coupled with the performance analysis of the building helps the owner and occupants to make informed decisions on performance goals for future earthquakes. These may differ from those that have been established as the minimum through public policy. If repairs or upgrades to meet the objectives are not possible immediately, owners or occupants can develop contingency plans to respond and recover more effectively from future earthquakes.

5. Incorporate seismic performance objectives, and related required repairs and modifications to meet them, into the long-term facility planning and replacement process. Buildings and their systems and furnishings deteriorate over time. Additionally, the programmatic needs of the owner or occupant also evolve. Modifications to improve seismic performance should fall into essentially the same category, unless extraordinary life safety problems are found.

3.12 Summary

The performance-based procedures for the evaluation of damage presented in FEMA 306 (ATC, 1998a) and the repair issues and procedures discussed in this document offer several technical improvements that support effective engineering standards and policy for repair and upgrading.

First, these methods provide a technically sound framework for earthquake damage evaluation and repair. The distortions and damage of the individual components relate directly to the global displacement of the structure. For a given movement at the roof level, for example, there is an associated damage state for each building component. This damage state implies a level of performance capacity as a function of the global displacement. Consequently, the displacement demand associated with a specific intensity of earthquake shaking defines a corresponding specific level of damage for the building.

Second, the global analysis procedure relies on a theoretical model built from the individual components of the structure. In the past, there has been a concern on the part of engineers that the repair, strengthening, or replacement of individual components and/or the addition of new components or elements might impose critical future damage on other parts of the structure. The proposed analytical technique allows the engineer to evaluate directly these potential adverse effects. A compilation of available information in FEMA 307 (ATC, 1998b) and this document summarizes the state of knowledge on the behavior of individual components of concrete and masonry wall buildings, including the effects of damage and repair. Although the available component data are by no means complete, the proposed procedures and criteria provide a conceptual protocol for compiling and using data that become available in the future.

Finally, the performance-based formulation provides relevant measurement devices to assess the effects of damage and other parameters that are useful in developing and implementing private and public policy for evaluation, repair, and upgrading of buildings. These devices are flexible enough to accommodate the tolerance of the individual community for risk, the selection of building-specific performance objectives, coordination of seismic performance with other public and private goals, and other important considerations.

When selecting performance objectives, consideration should be made of the possibility that damage may affect future performance in events of a smaller magnitude than the event that caused the damage. Specifically, some damage may decrease the stiffness of the building without significantly affecting its performance in larger events; however, the loss of stiffness may result in larger displacements and greater damage in smaller events than would have occurred in the pre-event structure.

4. Implementation

4.1 Introduction

Once a policy decision has been made on the appropriate action to take with an earthquake-damaged building (accept, restore, or upgrade), a design professional may need to develop a repair design. As noted previously, repair design has been hampered by a lack of truly applicable standards. Furthermore, the effectiveness of specific repair technologies has been poorly documented. This section summarizes a performance-based approach that uses emerging technologies. Additionally, some practical information on the specification of repairs for concrete and masonry wall buildings is tabulated.

4.2 Performance-Based Repair Design

Performance-based procedures for the evaluation and retrofit of existing buildings, FEMA 273/274 (ATC, 1997a, b) and ATC-40 (ATC, 1996), are technically similar. The FEMA 273 *Guidelines*, which are written in a style similar to a building code, and its companion FEMA 274 *Commentary* apply to any building type. The scope of ATC-40 emphasizes concrete buildings, but also includes extensive discussion of the evaluation and retrofit process that can be applied to all building types. It is written in textbook style.

The FEMA 273 and ATC-40 documents provide procedures to evaluate the anticipated performance of an existing building and to develop design measures to improve performance. These procedures can be readily adapted to the repair of earthquake-damaged buildings using this document and FEMA 306 and FEMA 307. The evaluation process for damaged concrete and masonry wall buildings is covered extensively in FEMA 306.

The use of performance-based procedures for repair design for a damaged building is actually just a special case of a retrofit of an existing building. The process is briefly reviewed here:

1. Select an appropriate performance objective for the building. For an upgrade, the goal would be to repair the building in such a way that its repaired performance index, P^*, for the specific objective is equal to or greater than 1.0. In the case of a restoration, the goal would be to implement repairs to return the building to its pre-event performance index for that specific objective ($P^* \approx P$).

2. Develop a repair strategy at the component level. Actions might include repairing individual components to restore their structural properties, removing and replacing damaged components, or adding new components in other locations. In some cases, damaged components might be left unrepaired.

3. Generate a global capacity curve representative of the building in its repaired condition. This requires the selection of appropriate component properties for damaged, repaired, or new components. For concrete and masonry wall buildings, FEMA 306 and FEMA 307 provide extensive guidance.

4. Using the procedures of FEMA 306, determine whether the repair strategy allows the repaired building to meet the performance objective. If not, revise or modify the strategy and repeat Steps 3 and 4.

5. Develop design drawings and specifications for the repair strategy. Section 4.3 summarizes repair technologies for concrete and masonry wall buildings. For the design of new components, the recommendations of FEMA 273/274, ATC 40, and conventional design standards are appropriate.

4.3 Repair Technologies

This section provides guidance on the specification of individual repair techniques applicable to the components of earthquake-damaged concrete and masonry wall buildings. The scope of repairs for an individual element or for an entire building depends on the objectives of the repair program.

4.3.1 Categories of Repairs

Repairs for earthquake-damaged concrete and masonry wall buildings fall into three generic categories:

1. *Cosmetic Repairs* are those repairs that improve the visual appearance of component damage. These repairs may also restore the nonstructural properties of the component, such as weather protection. Any structural benefit is negligible. An example is the routing, sealing, and painting of cracks in concrete or masonry.

2. *Structural Repairs* address component damage directly, with the intent to restore structural properties. Examples include injection of cracks or the replacement of fractured reinforcing bars.

3. *Structural Enhancements* are repairs that comprise supplemental additions, or removal and replacement of existing damaged components. They also include the addition of new components in the structure not necessarily at the site of existing damaged components. In this case, the intent is to replace structural properties of damaged components rather than to restore them. Examples include the application of concrete overlays to damaged walls or the addition of shear walls or steel bracing to the building where these elements and components were not present before the earthquake.

Table 4-1 is a list of repairs by category identifying the applicability of the repair to individual components, according to material and framing type.

4.3.2 Nonstructural Considerations

This document focuses on the structural performance of individual components. In practice, the restoration or upgrading of a damaged building is a program of repairs applied globally. The broader program perspective gives rise to a number of other critical issues.

- The efficiency associated with the structural repairs must be considered at the global level. For example, a given component might be most effectively repaired using a particular procedure; however, an alternative procedure might lead to overall lower costs when architectural or other constraints are considered.

- The historic status of the building must be considered when developing the repair program. Some repair procedures may not satisfy preservation goals for the building.

- Local building departments may have restrictions or requirements for certain repair procedures.

Table 4-1   Summary of repair procedures

Repair Category	Material			Repair ID	Repair Type
	Reinf. Concrete	Reinf. Masonry	URM		
Cosmetic Repair	√	√	√	CR 1	Surface coating
			√	CR 2	Repointing
	√	√*		CR 3	Crack injection with epoxy
Structural Repair	√	√*		SR 1	Crack injection with epoxy
	√	√	√	SR 2	Crack injection with grout
	√	√		SR 3	Spall repair
	√			SR 4	Rebar replacement
	√	√	√	SR 5	Wall replacement
Structural Enhancement	√	√	√	SE 1	Concrete overlay
	√	√	√	SE 2	Composite Fibers
	√			SE 3	Crack Stitching

Notes: Repairs for concrete walls can also be used for concrete frames in infilled frame systems.

Repairs for steel frames of infill systems are described in the component repair guides.

* Epoxy injection not recommended for partially-grouted reinforced masonry.

4.3.3 Repair Guides

The Repair Guides at the end of this section provide outline specifications for typical repair procedures for earthquake-damaged concrete and masonry wall buildings. These have been developed in conjunction with procedures for evaluating earthquake damage specifically for these building types. The Repair Guides themselves may be applicable, in whole or in part, to other building types, depending on specific circumstances. Many other repair techniques useful for other building types are not documented here.

The Repair Guides describe procedures that have been used routinely in the past for concrete and masonry components. There are undoubtedly other repair techniques that may also be applicable in general or in specific instances. Often, repair procedures need to be adapted to actual field conditions. The Repair Guides convey the basic information for repair selection on a conceptual level. They are not complete specifications and should not be used directly as construction documents. The design engineer must adapt these general repairs to meet the requirements of each building and component.

Each guide includes the following information:

Repair Name and ID	For reference and identification
Repair Category	Cosmetic repair, structural repair, or structural enhancement
Materials	Applicability to reinforced concrete, reinforced masonry, or unreinforced masonry
Description	Basic overview of the objectives and scope of the repair procedure
Repair Materials	Typical products used for the repair
Equipment	A summary of the tools, instrumentation, or devices required
Execution	General sequence of operations
Quality Assurance	Measures required to achieve satisfactory installation
Limitations	Restrictions on the effectiveness of the repair
Standards and References	Applicable sources of further information

	REPAIR GUIDE	Repair Type:	Cosmetic Repair
CR 1	**COSMETIC PATCHING**	**Materials:**	Concrete, Reinforced Masonry, Unreinforced Masonry

Description

A cosmetic patch consists of applying a surface coating on the surface of the concrete or masonry wall to conceal the surface projection of cracks. The purpose of patching is to improve the aesthetic appearance of the wall or to provide an additional barrier against water infiltration into the wall. Restoration of the fire resistance of a wall may also be required. Alternately, repair or installation of architectural finishes covering the wall is another method of cosmetic patching. Surface coatings in such repairs are not intended to provide any increase in strength or stiffness to the wall.

Repair Materials

Various materials can be used for surface coatings. The choice of repair material will depend on the functional and architectural requirements. Some examples of materials are:

- Paint can be used to conceal fine cracks on the surfaces of concrete and reinforced masonry walls

- Wall coverings such as wallpaper can be used on smooth interior concrete surfaces

- Dry-wall taping compound can be used to fill cracks on interior surfaces before paint or wall coverings are are applied

- Organic polymer materials can be used to fill cracks on interior and exterior concrete or reinforced masonry surfaces

- Coatings or sealers can be used on cracks on exterior surfaces to reduce water penetration for concrete, reinforced masonry, and unreinforced masonry walls

- Portland cement plaster can be applied to the surface to cover the appearance of cracks in concrete, reinforced masonry, or unreinforced masonry walls

- Cracks that need to be sealed only to prevent water intrusion can be injected with urethane

Equipment

The equipment required to apply the various repair materials are generally available tools such as mixing equipment and sprayers.

Execution

The owner or responsible party should choose a proper material for the surface coating. The choice of material should be based on the functional requirements of the wall, architectural considerations, and considerations of the historic nature of the building, if applicable.

Prior to implementing the repair, a test area should be prepared using the contractor, equipment, procedures, and materials to be used for the project. The completed mock-up should be allowed to cure and then carefully reviewed to verify that the appearance will match that of the surrounding walls.

The surfaces to receive the coatings should be properly prepared to ensure adequate bonding between the new and existing materials. For paint or wall-covering application, the surface of the wall should be clean and free of loose materials. Surface coatings such as plaster or water-resistant coatings should typically receive a light sand blasting to remove the existing coating and to provide a rougher surface for improved bonding.

COSMETIC PATCHING
continued

Quality Assurance
Paint or film-forming surface coatings or membranes exposed to moisture should be checked for adhesion to the existing surface.

Limitations
Paint can be used to bridge small cracks, with some paints capable of bridging cracks up to 0.06 inch. The manufacturer of the paint should be consulted for determining the capabilities and required preparation for the specific application.

The surface coatings listed can be effective at preventing water intrusion through cracks in exterior walls. However, these materials are only appropriate if the crack is dormant. Cracks caused by earthquake loading are typically dormant since they will not change in width over time. If the crack was caused by shrinkage, temperature movements, or other reasons, these treatments will not be effective at bridging the cracks. Therefore, the engineer must be confident that the earthquake caused the crack. Active or moving cracks that are to be watertight must be routed out and sealed with a flexible sealant.

Portland cement stucco plaster can be applied directly to a concrete or masonry surface. Since the existing wall is rigid and the new stucco coating will tend to exhibit drying shrinkage, shrinkage cracks may develop in the stucco. If the surface of the wall is not expected to produce adequate bond to the stucco, mechanical anchorage of the stucco to the wall should be specified (PCA, 1988).

Walls that had a designated fire rating may have the fire resistance compromised by cracks that extend through the thickness of the wall, since the cracks will allow hot combustion gases to pass through the wall. Epoxy injection will fill the cracks, but the heat from a fire will cause epoxy to melt. Testing has shown that unprotected concrete walls with epoxy-filled cracks up to ¼-inch wide could have about 3 inches of the epoxy burned out during a standard fire (Plecnick and Pham, 1980). The burned-out epoxy can be cleaned out and the crack re-injected. A final plaster coating on the wall can significantly reduce epoxy burnout.

References
PCA, 1988, *Portland Cement Plaster (Stucco) Manual*, Portland Cement Association, Skokie, Illinois.

Plecnick, J.M. and M.G. Pham, 1980, *Final Report on Fire Testing of Epoxy Repaired Shear Walls*, Structures Laboratory Report # SL80-7-11, California State University, Long Beach, Long Beach, California.

	REPAIR GUIDE	Repair Type:	Cosmetic Repair
CR 2	**REPOINTING MORTAR**	Materials:	Reinforced Masonry, Unreinforced Masonry

Purpose

Repointing is the process of removing deteriorated mortar from the joints of a masonry wall and replacing it with new mortar. Repointing may be required to repair earthquake-damaged mortar joints or to repair deterioration of mortar joints caused by weathering. Properly installed repointing restores the visual and physical integrity of the masonry. Improperly installed repointing can detract from the appearance of the building and can cause physical damage to the masonry.

A method known variously as "grouting," "scrub coats," "slurry coats," or "slur coats" is sometimes sold as a substitute for repointing. The process involves brushing a thin coat of mortar over all masonry units and joints, and when the mortar is dry, brushing it off the masonry units. This technique has a life expectancy of only a few years, it masks the joint detailing or tooling, and the residue is difficult to remove from the masonry. This technique is not a substitute for repointing, and should never be used on historic buildings.

Repair Materials

The new (repointing) mortar should:

- match the existing mortar in color, texture, and detailing. The best way to match the color is by using sand similar in color, size and shape of grains as the original mortar. As the mortar weathers, the sand gives the mortar its characteristic color and texture. Pigments should not be used to match mortar color, unless matching cannot be achieved with sand, since pigments will fade over time.

- be softer, in terms of compressive stiffness, than the adjacent masonry units. A new mortar that is too hard will cause stresses in the wall (from thermal and moisture expansion and contraction, and settlement) to be accommodated by the masonry units rather than the mortar, causing cracking and spalling of the masonry.

- be as soft as or softer than the original mortar, in terms of compressive stiffness.

Many older historic buildings used a lime mortar. If a lime mortar was originally used, the building should be repointed with a lime mortar. New cement mortar should not be used, as it can cause deterioration of the wall by not allowing moisture out of the wall and by introducing salts. If a cement or cement-lime mortar was originally used, the building should be repointed with a similar mortar.

Masonry cement should not be used for repointing mortar. Appropriate mortar materials are as follows:

- Lime should conform to ASTM C207, Type S, Hydrated Lime for Masonry Purposes.

- Cement should conform to ASTM C150, Type I or II, low alkali, nonstaining Portland cement.

- Sand should conform to ASTM C144 to ensure proper gradation and freedom from impurities. Sand color, size, and texture should match the original as closely as possible.

- Water should be clean and free from significant amounts of acids, alkalis, or organic material.

The mortar mix for historic buildings should be specified by the preservation consultant. Generally, it should comply with the UBC Standard No. 24-9 (ICBO, 1994) and ASTM C270, *Standard Specification for Mortar for Unit Masonry*. Material proportions should be given by volume.

Mortar samples should be made before starting work on the building. Samples of the proposed mortar should be made, allowed to cure, then broken open. The broken surface of the new mortar should be compared with a broken surface of the original mortar to determine whether they match.

Equipment

In general, the old mortar should be removed using a hammer and cold chisel. Power saws should not be used as they can damage the adjacent masonry units. A dallett-style pneumatic carving tool can be used successfully by experienced masons to remove old mortar.

REPAIR GUIDE
continued

Execution

The contractor should demonstrate repointing on a test panel in an inconspicuous area of the building that includes all types of masonry, joint types, and problems to be encountered on the job. Usually a 3-foot by 6-foot test panel is sufficient. Once the test panel is approved, work can begin.

The joint is prepared by removing the mortar to a depth of 2 ½ times the width of the joints. For most masonry, this depth is ½ to 1 inch. Any loose or disintegrated mortar beyond this minimum depth should be removed. Care should be taken not to damage the existing adjacent masonry units. Loose material in the joints should be removed with a brush, and the joint flushed with a water stream.

The mortar is prepared by measuring all dry ingredients and mixing them together. When ready to use the mortar, add water to bring it to a consistency that is somewhat drier than conventional masonry mortar.

The joints should be damp, but with no standing water. Install new mortar only when temperature is between 4° and 95° F. During hot weather, repoint on the shady side of the building, or install netting over the scaffolding to provide shade. Mortar is packed into the joint in ¼-inch-thick layers, leaving no voids, until the joint is filled. Tool the joint to match the original mortar. If desired, after mortar has initially hardened, stipple with a brush to give a weathered appearance. Remove excess mortar from adjacent masonry using a bristle brush. Keep the pointing mortar damp for 2 to 3 days, using a fine-mist hand sprayer.

Quality Assurance

- Make sure that only damaged or deteriorated joints requiring it are repointed.
- Require samples of the repointing mortar to verify the mortar matches the original.
- Require test panels to verify the quality of workmanship and retain them throughout the job for comparison.
- Inspect joints after preparation to verify that enough old mortar has been removed.
- Make sure joints are dampened before application of new mortar.

- Make sure that joints are being tooled to match original appearance. Often, the corners of the masonry units are worn back and if the joints are completely filled to the surface, the joints will be considerably wider than original, ruining the appearance. If the corners of the masonry units are spalled or worn, the mortar will have to be slightly recessed in the joint to achieve the original appearance.

Limitations

The owner, consultant, and contractor should realize that repointing can be a time-consuming and expensive repair. (However, proper repointing is the only long-lasting repair for cracked or deteriorated mortar joints. A good repointing job can last up to 50 years.)

References

ASTM, 1997, *Standard Specification for Aggregate for Masonry Mortar, C144-97,* American Society for Testing and Materials, West Conshohocken, Pennsylvania.

ASTM, 1997, *Standard Specification for Portland Cement, C150-97a,* American Society for Testing and Materials, West Conshohocken, Pennsylvania.

ASTM, 1997, *Standard Specification for Hydrated Lime for Masonry Purposes, C207-97,* American Society for Testing and Materials, West Conshohocken, Pennsylvania.

ASTM, 1997, *Standard Specification for Mortar for Unit Masonry, C270-97,* American Society for Testing and Materials, West Conshohocken, Pennsylvania.

ICBO, 1994, *Pointing of Unreinforced Masonry Walls,* Uniform Building Code Standard No. 24-9, International Conference of Building Officials, Whittier, California.

Mack, R.C., T.P Tiller, & J.S. Askins., 1980, *Preservations Briefs: 2 Repointing Mortar Joints in Historic Brick Buildings,* U. S. Depart of the Interior, Heritage Conservation and Recreation Service, Technical Preservation Services Division, U. S. Government Printing Office, Washington, D.C.

REPAIR GUIDE	Repair Type:	Cosmetic Repair Structural Repair
CR 3/SR 1 CRACK INJECTION - EPOXY	Materials:	Concrete Reinforced Masonry

Purpose

Crack injection consists of applying a structural binding agent into a crack for the purpose of filling the crack and adhering to the substrate material. Various types of materials and methods can be used for crack injection depending on the required performance. For concrete and fully-grouted, reinforced masonry walls, epoxy is typically injected into cracks under pressure.

Repair Materials

* ASTM Standard C881, Type I, low-viscosity grade epoxy.

* Other materials such as fine cementitious grout and urethanes can also be used for structural bonding.

Equipment

* Pressure injection machine with mixing nozzle at the tip capable of injecting with pressures of 300 psi.

* Porting devices installed with specialized drill bits.

* Equipment to monitor pressure and mixing.

Execution

Prior to injection, loose material should be removed from the cracks. Cracks can be injected through surface-mounted ports or into drilled entry ports, although surface-mounted ports are used by most contractors (Krauss et al., 1995). The injection ports are located along the length of the crack and should be spaced at a distance roughly equal to the thickness of the wall, depending on the viscosity of the material and the manufacturer's recommendations. Ports should be drilled with drills that prevent fines from remaining in the crack. When full-thickness repairs are required, it is beneficial to seal both surfaces of the wall along the crack, except for the entry ports. When epoxy injection is for cosmetic purposes or when less than full-thickness repairs are acceptable, the crack is sealed only on the injection side.

Before injecting, the epoxy should be pumped into a paper cup until the material appears to be completely mixed. Cracks are injected starting at the bottom of vertical and diagonal cracks, changing to the next port as the epoxy appears there. Splitting tubes can be used so that the epoxy can be pumped into multiple ports simultaneously. Previously injected ports should be sealed. If necessary, the surface is ground smooth to remove the surface seal and leakage after the epoxy has set. Grinding should not be started until the epoxy has cured.

Quality Assurance

Personnel experienced in epoxy injection should be used for the work. The mixing equipment should be evaluated before beginning the work to verify proper operation. Samples should be prepared and tested for consistency of the epoxy and bond strength. Twice daily during the epoxy work, the mix ratio should be tested to ensure it is within the manufacturer's tolerances. The mix test should be conducted at the pressures at which the work is being done.

The effectiveness of crack injection can be confirmed by alternative methods. These methods, however, only test the penetration of the epoxy into the cracks; they do not check the adequacy of the bond of the epoxy to the substrate.

Core holes can be drilled through the cracks after injection and visually examined to verify that the epoxy has penetrated the cracks. Typically, 2-inch diameter core holes are specified. The spacing of the core holes should be between 50 feet and 100 feet (Trout, 1991)

Nondestructive evaluation methods can be used to verify the effectiveness of the epoxy penetration (Guedelhoefer and Krauklis,1986).

REPAIR GUIDE
continued

Limitations

Moisture on the crack surface can reduce the bond of the epoxy to the crack faces. If the crack contains contaminants, it should be cleaned to remove both the contaminants and any moisture that will reduce the bond.

Crack widths as small as 0.002 inch in width can be injected with epoxy. Crack widths up to 0.012 inch can be tolerated in reinforced concrete in humid or moist air conditions (ACI, 1994a). A low-viscosity epoxy will not be effective for crack widths greater than 1/8 inch. For widths greater than 1/8 inch a medium-viscosity epoxy should be used. For surface crack widths greater than ¼ inch, epoxy pastes or gels should be used. For cracks that are wider at the surface, an epoxy paste can be applied at the surface and a low-viscosity epoxy injected through the cured paste to the smaller, interior cracks.

Epoxy injection can also restore the bond of reinforcing bars (French et al., 1990). For the epoxy to restore the bond, there needs to be a sufficient amount of surface cracking that intersects the debonded reinforcing for the epoxy to penetrate along the surface of the reinforcing bar.

The operator must be attentive to the amount of epoxy being injected relative to the spacing of the ports. A theoretical quantity of epoxy to be used can be calculated. Injection should stop if the amount required exceeds 50 percent more than the calculated amount (ACI, 1994b). This is particularly important when injecting reinforced masonry walls that may contain large voids. Excessive amounts of epoxy may also indicate that epoxy is leaking out through a crack or joint.

If the ports are spaced too far apart for the viscosity of the epoxy, the epoxy may harden before reaching the adjacent port. Conversely, if the ports are too closely spaced, the epoxy may not reach the full thickness of the wall before bleeding out of the adjacent port.

After finding satisfactory penetration from a number of cores, the spacing of subsequent cores can by increased,

provided the same operator, epoxy, and equipment are used and the environmental and structural conditions remain the same.

Nondestructive evaluation (NDE) methods should be used on the cracked wall prior to repairs and should be calibrated for the repaired condition using undamaged sections of wall. However, NDE methods may not be effective in evaluating the penetration into small cracks.

References

ACI Committee 224R, 1994a, "Control of Cracking in Concrete Structures" *ACI Manual of Concrete Practice*, Detroit, Michigan.

ACI Committee 503R, 1994b, Use of Epoxy Compounds with Concrete", *ACI Manual of Concrete Practice*, Detroit, Michigan.

ASTM, 1990, *Standard Specification for Epoxy-Resin-Base Bonding Systems for Concrete, C881-90*, American Society for Testing and Materials, West Conshohocken, Pennsylvania.

French, C.W. et al, 1990, "Epoxy Repair Techniques for Moderate Earthquake Damage", *ACI Structural Journal*, July-August 1990, American Concrete Institute, Detroit, Michigan, pp 416-424.

Guedelhoefer, O.C. and A.T. Krauklis, 1986, "To Bond Or Not To Bond", *Concrete International*, August 1986, Detroit, Michigan, pp. 10- 15.

Krauss, P.D, et al, 1995, *Evaluation of Injection Materials for the Repair of Deep Cracks in Concrete Structures*, Technical Report REMR-CS-48, US Army Corps of Engineers, Washington, DC.

Trout, J.F., 1991, "Quality Control on the Injection Project", *Concrete International*, December 1991, American Concrete Institute, Detroit, Michigan, pp 50-52.

	REPAIR GUIDE	**Repair Type:**	Structural Repair
SR 2	**CRACK INJECTION - GROUT**	**Materials:**	Concrete, Reinforced Masonry, Unreinforced Masonry

Description

Where cracks along the mortar joints in unreinforced masonry walls produce horizontal offsets in the plane of the wall, the cracks can be repaired by injection of fine grout into the cracks. The grout fills the cracks with material that bonds to the masonry. The grout can also fill voids within the wall, such as in the collar joint. If the bond of the grout is at least equal to the bond of the original mortar, the repaired wall will have at least the same strength and stiffness as the pre-earthquake condition. Since the grout can also fill pre-existing voids within the wall, some improvement may be realized, but should not be expected.

Repair Materials

The material used for injection is grout. Removable loose bricks will require mortar. The grout is typically composed of sand, portland cement, lime, and fly ash. Recommended proportions are presented by the City of Los Angeles Rule of General Application (RGA) No. 1-91 (City of LA, 1991). Variations may be required based on local material availability and other requirements.

Other proportions and materials can be used. It is recommended that the materials and proportions be verified for use in the subject application by testing before implementation.

Equipment

The following equipment is typically required to perform this work: mixing equipment and pump, pressure-monitoring system. Additional equipment may be necessary, depending on the local conditions. A rotary drill with masonry bits with vacuum chucks is useful in preventing dust from accumulating in the hole.

Execution

The walls are prepared by removing loose mortar from open joints. The cracks are flushed with water and then filled with pre-hydrated mortar, which is tooled to match the existing joints. Loose bricks should be removed and reset with mortar.

Injection holes are drilled at head joints or cracked brick, through to the inner wythe in each course, although not entering any air space. Verification ports are drilled 8 to 12 inches to each side of the injection holes. The holes are flushed with water.

Grout is mixed and then pumped into the holes. Typical pressures are 10 to 30 psi. Injection should start at the bottom and work upwards. Grout is injected at a port until grout flows from the adjacent holes. All of the holes along a horizontal joint are filled before moving to the next higher mortar joint.

When the grout has set, the holes are pointed with mortar.

REPAIR GUIDE
continued

Quality Assurance

For work within the City of Los Angeles, contractors performing grout injection must be certified by the department of Building and Safety. The certification process is described in the RGA and generally involves a meeting with an Earthquake Repair Inspector and a demonstration of the procedure (City of Los Angeles, 1991).

To perform the grouting properly, the work requires a minimum crew of two certified persons; one as a foreman, and one as a nozzleman. The foreman is responsible for coordination, verifying the pressure of the grout, and batching the grout. The nozzleman is responsible for operating the injection nozzle at the wall.

Before injecting grout, all of the injection and verification holes should be inspected to verify the depth of the holes. During the injection, the grout mixture and injection pressure should be continuously monitored for conformance with the specifications. The verification holes should be watched to verify that the grout is filling the voids. After injecting, core holes should be drilled and visually inspected to verify that the grout filled the voids.

Limitations

This procedure has been demonstrated to be effective for cracks ranging from 0.007 inch wide up to ¾ inch wide. Epoxy resins are not recommended for injection into masonry since the properties of the epoxy will not be compatible with those of the masonry. Admixtures such as superplasticizers can aid in the fluidity of the grout so that the grout fills more of the voids.

Existing grout in the collar joints will prevent some dispersion of the injected grout. Crack injection with grout may not restore all of the compressive strength of the masonry, since the grout may not penetrate all of the micro-cracks (Manzouri et al., 1996).

Increasing the pump pressure is not effective at increasing the distance of dispersion of the grout from the injection port (Kariotis and Roselund, 1987). The dispersion can be increased by increasing the fluidity of the grout mixture.

References

City of Los Angeles, 1991, "Crack Repair Of Unreinforced Masonry Walls With Grout Injection," *Rule of General Application - RGA No. 1-91.*

Kariotis, J.C and N.A Roselund, 1987, "Repair of Earthquake Damage to Unreinforced Masonry Buildings," *Evaluation and Retrofit of Masonry Structures*, Proceedings of the Second USA-Italy Workshop on Evaluation and Retrofit of Masonry Structures, pp 201-214.

Manzouri, T., M.P. Schuller, P.B. Shing, and B Amadei, 1996, Repair and Retrofit of Unreinforced Masonry Structures, *Earthquake Spectra*, Vol. 12, No. 4, Earthquake Engineering Research Institute, Oakland, California, pp 903-922.

SR 3	REPAIR GUIDE	Repair Type:	Structural Repair
	SPALL REPAIR	Materials:	Concrete Reinforced Masonry, Unreinforced Masonry

Description

Spalls are small sections of wall that become loose or dislodged. Spalls can occur in both concrete and masonry walls. The missing material is replaced with a suitable patch. The material used for the patch must have structural and thermal properties similar to the existing material. The materials and procedures for the patch will also depend on the size and location of the spall and the wall material. These spall repair procedure can be used for concrete, reinforced masonry, infill materials, and unreinforced masonry walls.

Repair Materials

For concrete and reinforced masonry walls, the repair material is typically a repair mortar mix, which can be based on inorganic materials, such as Portland cement and latex-modified concrete, or organic materials, such as epoxy and polyester. The mortar mix will include sand and may also include pea gravel. For thick repairs, a mechanical anchorage, using epoxy-embedded dowels, may need to be added to secure the patch.

Equipment

The following equipment is typically required:

- Chipping hammer and grinders or concrete saws
- Mixing and placing tools

Execution

The concrete or reinforced masonry wall should have all loose material removed with chipping hammers to expose sound substrate. If reinforcing bars are significantly exposed, the concrete or grout should be removed to provide sufficient clearance around the bar for the patch to bond to the full diameter. The perimeter of the spall should be cut with a saw or grinder to create an edge perpendicular to the original surface.

Shallow spall repairs are those that are less than about ¾ inch deep (Krauss, 1994). Deep spalls require correspondingly course aggregate to be added to the repair mortar. For large patches, new steel dowels should be set into the substrate with epoxy and placed so that they extend into the patch.

The substrate should be prepared in accordance with the recommendations of the manufacturer. Separate bonding agents do not generally have to be applied to the surface. The mortar is first scrubbed onto the surface with a stiff broom or brush and then applied with a trowel in lifts. The surface is finished to match the appearance of the original wall surface. The patch is then cured in accordance with manufacturer's recommendations.

REPAIR GUIDE
continued

SR 3

Quality Assurance

Contractors conducting the repairs should be familiar with the repair materials and procedures. If proprietary mortars are specified, the contractor performing the repairs should be certified by the manufacturer of the mortar.

The most critical aspect of the performance of a patch is the bond of the repair material to the substrate (Holl and O'Connor, 1997). The bond strength can be evaluated by a pull-off test, as described in ACI 503R (ACI, 1994). The quality of the bond can also be assessed using nondestructive testing techniques such as Impact Echo or SASW.

Limitations

When patching spalls in unreinforced masonry walls and infill frame walls, it may be difficult to obtain repair materials that have properties similar to the masonry. The repairs may also need to consider the changes to the appearance of the wall due to the patch. Mock-up tests should be conducted to verify the applicability of the repairs prior to wide-spread use throughout a building.

These spall repair procedures are suitable for most spalls in concrete or reinforced masonry that are up to ½ cubic foot in volume. Larger spalls in concrete walls may require using formwork and portland cement concrete as the patch material or by the use of shotcrete. Large spalls in reinforced and unreinforced masonry walls may require removing damaged masonry units and replacing them with new, similar units.

Most repair mortars will experience some shrinkage after curing. Therefore, a visible crack may develop around the patch. If the appearance of this crack will be unacceptable, a nonshrink grout mixture should be used or provisions made to conduct cosmetic repairs several days or weeks later.

References

ACI Committee 503, 1994, "Use of Epoxy Compounds with Concrete", ACI 503R-93, *ACI Manual of Concrete Practice*, American Concrete Institute, Detroit, Michigan.

Holl, C.H and Scott O'Connor, 1997, "Cleaning and Preparing Concrete before Repair", *Concrete International*, March 1997, American Concrete Institute, Detroit, Michigan, pp 60-63.

Krauss, P.D. 1994, *Repair Materials and Techniques for Concrete Structures in Nuclear Power Plants*, NRC JNC No. B8045, US Nuclear Regulatory Commission, Washington, DC.

	REPAIR GUIDE	Repair Type:	Structural Repair
SR 4	REBAR REPLACEMENT	Materials:	Concrete Reinforced Masonry

Description

Mechanical connections can be used in lieu of conventional lapped bar splices to connect or splice two pieces of reinforcing bar. Mechanical connections are particularly useful for connecting new bars to existing bars already embedded in a masonry or concrete structure. They are also useful for repairing damaged structures. Where fractures have occurred in reinforcing bars, or where conventional lapped bar splices have failed, it may be possible to repair the discontinuity by means of a mechanical connection. When repairing certain types of damage, it is necessary to cut out the damaged length of reinforcing bar and to replace it with new bar. In this instance, two mechanical connections are required, where one connection is installed at each end of the replacement bar.

Repair Materials

The materials used to make a mechanical connection include the mechanical connection device itself, obtained from the splice manufacturer, and the reinforcing bar being connected. Some mechanical connections use a filler material, such as cementitious grout or a molten metal, typically provided by the splice manufacturer. Most mechanical devices can be used with either ASTM A615 or ASTM A706 reinforcing bar. Certain devices require use of reinforcing bar provided by the splice manufacturer.

Numerous types and configurations of proprietary mechanical connections are available from several different manufacturers. Mechanical connection configurations include:

- Cold-swaged sleeves
- Grout-filled sleeves
- Steel-filled sleeves
- Upset-and-threaded couplers
- Tapered-threaded couplers
- Sleeve with wedge
- Sleeve with lock screws

These and other devices are further described in ACI 439.3R-9, *Mechanical Connections of Reinforcing Bars*, by Committee 439 of the American Concrete Institute (ACI) and also in *Reinforcement Anchorages and Splices*, by the Concrete Reinforcing Steel Institute (CRSI). Detailed technical information is obtained from the proprietary manufacturers.

Equipment

Many proprietary connections can be assembled using readily-available hand or power tools, such as ordinary wrenches, calibrated wrenches, or non-impact torque wrenches. Assembly of some connector devices requires special equipment such as an hydraulic press. Tools required vary with the type of connection. The splice manufacturer should be consulted for specific equipment requirements.

REPAIR GUIDE
continued

SR 4

Execution

Unless threaded, the reinforcing bars to be connected need no special preparation beyond a clean-cut end. Connections to bars embedded in masonry require limited removal of some surrounding masonry in order to provide room for insertion of the splice device (but the volume of masonry removed to make a mechanical connection is generally less than that required to make a conventional lapped bar splice). Generally, bars can be set loosely into place, with final alignment made just before completing the splice assembly. The final completion of the connection is carried out in accordance with the instructions provided by the manufacturer.

Quality Assurance

Prior to completing final assembly of the connection, it should be verified that the proper length of reinforcing bar has been inserted into the splice device and that the bars are correctly aligned. There are also other quality assurance checks that will vary depending upon the particular type of connection being used. For example, with grout-filled sleeve splices, the slump of the grout mixture should be measured. Again, the manufacturer should be consulted for detailed instruction regarding quality assurance.

For work within the City of Los Angeles, mechanical connection devices must have a General Approval issued by the Department of Building and Safety. As part of the approval process, a series of cyclic tests and tensile strength tests are carried out on sample mechanical connections. The application for General Approval is typically undertaken by the manufacturer of the mechanical connection in advance of any use of the product within the City of Los Angeles. However, the use of non-preapproved devices may be permitted on a case-by-case basis, upon submission of acceptable test data to the Department of Building and Safety.

For mechanical connection of reinforcing bars subject to inelastic cyclic loading, such as bars in or adjacent to a potential or actual plastic-hinge zone, it is also recommended that inelastic cyclic test data be provided by the device manufacturer. The test data should graphically illustrate the load-deflection behavior of the connector-and-bar system under repeated inelastic load cycles, and the post-cycling residual tensile strength of the system should approach or exceed the specified tensile strength of the unspliced reinforcing bar. The proposed ACI Standard includes such testing and strength criteria.

Limitations

There are some limitations on the use of mechanical splices, but a limitation for one device may not apply to a different device. Threaded devices are generally not suitable for connections involving existing bars embedded in concrete because the embedded bar cannot be threaded. The physical size of some devices may prevent their use in the occasional application with tight size constraints.

References

ACI Committee 439, In Progress, *Standard Specification for Mechanical Reinforcement Splices for Seismic Designs using Energy Dissipation Criteria, ACI 439*, American Concrete Institute, Detroit, Michigan.

ASTM, 1996, *Standard Specification for Deformed and Plain Billet-Steel Bars for Concrete Reinforcement, A615/A615M-96a*, American Society for Testing and Materials, West Conshohocken, Pennsylvania.

ASTM, 1996, *Standard Specification for Low-Alloy Steel Deformed and Plain Bars for Concrete Reinforcement, A706/A706M-96b*, American Society for Testing and Materials, West Conshohocken, Pennsylvania.

	REPAIR GUIDE	Repair Type:	Structural Repair
SR 5	**WALL REPLACEMENT**	Materials:	Concrete Reinforced Masonry, Unreinforced Masonry

Description

Wall replacement requires the removal of an existing wall and replacement with a new wall. The removal of the existing wall should be performed carefully so that the existing reinforcing bars, if present, can be spliced to new reinforcing. The construction of the new wall should match, as closely as possible, the construction of the existing wall.

Repair Materials

For concrete replacement walls, the strength of the concrete should be specified to be at least 3000 psi.

For reinforced masonry walls, open-ended units should be specified. These will allow easier installation within the existing structure. The masonry units, mortar, and grout used should conform to the requirements of ACI 530/ASCE 6.

Equipment

The equipment used will depend on the construction of the existing wall and the methods used to install the new wall. The following are general equipment items that might be needed for removal and replacement of walls:

- Chipping tools for removal of the wall
- Light chipping tools for preparing the surface of the remaining structure
- Equipment for mixing and placing the concrete, grout, or mortar

Execution

If the existing wall is a load-bearing wall, shoring must be installed adjacent to the wall to support the gravity loads while the wall is missing.

The existing wall is carefully removed using saws and chipping tools. Around the perimeter of the opening, care should be exercised to avoid damaging the remaining portions of the structure and to avoid damaging the reinforcing bars, if present.

The surface of the surrounding structure should be prepared for the new material. For concrete and reinforced masonry, the surface of the structure should be roughened to an amplitude of ¼ inch (ACI, 1995).

New reinforcing bars should be spliced to existing bars. If new reinforcing bars are required to be attached to the existing structure, these bars should be anchored to the existing structure by setting them into holes with epoxy. The depth of the hole should be sufficient to develop the strength of the bar. The manufacturer of the epoxy should be consulted for the proper depth of the bar and for the instructions for installing the epoxy.

The new concrete can be placed by forming the wall or by applying shotcrete. Shotcrete application should follow the guidelines for shotcrete overlays (SE1). For cast-in-place walls, concrete is placed through an access hole near the top of the formwork. Additional holes are required for inserting vibrators.

Cast-in-place concrete walls should be wet cured following placement. A curing compound should be used following the wet cure.

The cementitious materials in the new wall will experience drying shrinkage. Since the existing structure will not shrink, the shrinkage will cause a crack to form, typically along the top of the wall. After a significant amount of the drying shrinkage has occurred, typically after two to four months, the crack should be filled with epoxy.

REPAIR GUIDE
continued

Following rebar installation, open-ended masonry units can be installed around the reinforcing bars. When the height of the lift of grout is more than 5 feet, holes are left at the top and bottom for installation of grout. If open-ended units are used, access holes are needed every 2 to 3 feet. If closed-end units are used, cleanouts are needed for each cavity. Grout is pumped in through a hole in the top of the wall. The hole at the base is used to verify that the grout has flowed down to the base. After grout is observed at the bottom hole, the hole is sealed to prevent the grout from flowing out of the wall.

Quality Assurance
The mix design for the concrete, grout, or mortar should be submitted by the contractor and reviewed prior to use. Concrete core samples should be required from each batch of concrete used. The cores should be tested in accordance with ASTM C39 (ACI, 1995). Masonry units should be tested in accordance with the appropriate standards referenced in ACI 530/ASCE 6-92 (ACI, 1992). Concrete masonry units should be tested using ASTM C140. Brick should be tested using ASTM C 67.

The layout and anchorage of the reinforcing steel should be inspected before forming the concrete or installing the masonry units. A special inspector familiar with epoxy installation should observe installation of the epoxy. A percentage of the epoxy-anchored dowels should be load-tested to at least 50 percent of the yield strength of the bar.

Limitations
If the wall to be replaced was constructed with unreinforced masonry, the local building department may not allow replacement with a new unreinforced masonry wall. If the construction of the new wall is substantially different from the previous wall, the strength and stiffness behavior could adversely affect the performance of the building. It may be possible either to negotiate a compromise with the local building department or to introduce a weak link in the wall to prevent its increased stiffness or strength from affecting the behavior of the remainder of the building.

The shrinkage cracks that develop at the top of the wall, if not filled with epoxy or grout, will produce a weakened joint. This weakened joint may cause the behavior mode of the wall to be different from that of the original wall.

References
ACI Committee 530/ ASCE Committee 6, 1992, *Specifications for Masonry Structures*, American Society of Civil Engineers, New York, New York.

ACI Committee 318, 1995, *Building Code Requirements for Structural Concrete and Commentary*, American Concrete Institute, Detroit, Michigan.

ASTM, 1997, *Standard Test Methods for Sampling and Testing Brick and Structural Clay Tile, C67-97*, American Society for Testing and Materials, West Conshohocken, Pennsylvania.

ASTM, 1997, *Standard Test Methods of Sampling and Testing Concrete Masonry Units, C140-97*, American Society for Testing and Materials, West Conshohocken, Pennsylvania.

	REPAIR GUIDE	Repair Type:	Structural Enhancement
SE 1	**STRUCTURAL OVERLAY - CONCRETE**	**Materials:**	Concrete Reinforced Masonry, Unreinforced Masonry

Description

Overlay concrete is applied pneumatically (shotcrete) or as a cast-in-place layer onto one or both surfaces of the wall. The concrete is reinforced and attached to the existing structure to enable the concrete to provide supplemental strength to the wall. Two different processes for shotcrete are used in practice: wet mix and dry mix. In the wet-mix process, all ingredients are premixed and the wet mixture delivered to the nozzle where it is shot toward the surface. In the dry-mix process, the dry cement and aggregate are delivered to the nozzle where they are mixed with water while being shot out of the nozzle to the surface (Warner, 1995a).

Repair Materials

Portland cement, aggregate, and water are needed. The mixing and proportions will depend on a number of factors, including the process (wet-mix process or dry-mix process)

Equipment

The basic equipment includes a mixer, pump or gun, compressor, hoses, and nozzles. (ACI, 1994a, b)

Execution

The surface of the existing wall should be prepared by removing loose or damaged material. The surface should be chipped or scarified to avoid abrupt changes in dimension (ACI, 1994b). Reinforcing steel is installed and securely anchored into the existing slabs above and below using dowels set in epoxy.

Before applying the shotcrete, the surface of the existing wall should be prewetted so that specified shotcrete moisture content will not be absorbed into the existing wall (Warner, 1995b). Forms or guide wires are installed to provide alignment control for the application, finishing, and verification of sufficient cover for the reinforcing steel. The nozzleman should direct the shotcrete from the nozzle to the surface with a steady, uninterrupted flow. The angle of the nozzle should be kept as close as possible to perpendicular to the surface of the wall to reduce rebound. A slight angle is required when directing the shotcrete around reinforcing steel to avoid shadowing behind the bars. The shotcrete is applied in several passes starting at the base of the wall, building up the thickness slightly beyond the guide wires.

The shotcrete surface should be finished as required using the guide wires. The shotcrete should then be wet cured for at least one day and preferably seven days (Warner, 1995c). Following the wet cure, a final cure using liquid curing membranes, or other moisture-retaining coverings should be provided.

Quality Assurance

The quality of the shotcrete operation is highly dependent on the skill of the nozzleman. Each nozzleman used on a project should be certified and have sufficient experience in similar applications. The nozzlemen can be qualified by completing a large or full-scale mock-up test representing the thickness and congestion conditions that will be encountered.

The mix design for the shotcrete should be submitted by the contractor for review. Small test panels should be prepared in accordance with ASTM C1140, *Standard Practice for Preparing and Testing Specimens from Shotcrete Test Panels* (ASTM, 1997), by each nozzleman at the beginning of each day and at the start of each batch of shotcrete. The sample panels should be cured in the same manner as the walls. Core or cube samples should be removed from each panel and tested to verify the compressive strength and quality.

A qualified inspector should continuously inspect the shotcrete application. The inspector should verify that the materials, placement, finishing, and curing are conducted in accordance with the specifications.

REPAIR GUIDE
continued

SE 1

Limitations

The amount of reinforcing steel in the shotcrete wall should be kept to a minimum. This can be accomplished by using small bars, staggering bars when more than one layer of reinforcing is required (Warner, 1994), and using mechanical splices rather than lap splices. Excessive reinforcing prevents the shotcrete from being placed completely behind the reinforcing steel and also traps the rebound.

Shotcrete bonds well to clean concrete and masonry surfaces. The use of bonding agents is not recommended.

The wet-mix and dry-mix processes have different production requirements and require different skills of the operators. However, both can produce satisfactory results. The dry-mix process is capable of producing higher compressive strength, can be transported longer distances, and produces a material that generally has less shrinkage. The wet-mix process requires less skill of the nozzleman in order to mix uniformly the water with the cement and aggregate and is capable of greater production. The choice of which process to use depends on the capabilities and experience of the contractor.

An apprentice or blow man is recommended to be present to remove rebound, which is the aggregate and cement paste that bounces off the surface during shotcreting. The blowman should prevent the rebound from being mixed in with the shotcrete.

Reinforcing bars should generally not be larger than # 5 bars (ICBO, 1994). However, if larger bar sizes are required, the contractor should be required to perform mockup tests to demonstrate that the shotcrete can effectively be placed around the reinforcing bars. The mock-ups should be tested by core drilling or saw cutting samples at the reinforcing bars. The samples should then be visually analyzed to verify complete coverage of shotcrete around the bars. Full-time inspection of the shotcrete operation in the vicinity of the large bars is also recommended.

References

ACI, 1994a, "Guide to Shotcrete" ACI 506-90, *ACI Manual of Concrete Practice*, American Concrete Institute, Detroit, Michigan.

ACI, 1994b, "Specification for Shotcrete" ACI 506.2-90, *ACI Manual of Concrete Practice*, American Concrete Institute, Detroit, Michigan.

ASTM, 1997, *Standard Practice for Preparing and Testing Specimens from Shotcrete Test Panels, C1140-97*, American Society for Testing and Materials, West Conshohocken, Pennsylvania.

ICBO, 1994, *Uniform Building Code*, International Conference of Building Officials, Whittier, California.

Warner, James, 1994, "Shotcrete in Seismic Repair and Retrofit", *Seismic Rehabilitation of Concrete Structures*, ACI SP-160, American Concrete Institute, Detroit, Michigan.

Warner, James, 1995a, "Understanding Shotcrete - The Fundamentals", *Concrete International*, May 1995, American Concrete Institute, Detroit, Michigan, pp 59-64.

Warner, James, 1995b, "Understanding Shotcrete - Its Application", *Concrete International*, June 1995, American Concrete Institute, Detroit, Michigan, pp 37-41.

Warner, James, 1995, "Understanding Shotcrete - Finishing, Curing and Quality Control", *Concrete International*, August 1995, American Concrete Institute, Detroit, Michigan, pp 72-75.

	REPAIR GUIDE	Repair Type:	Structural Enhancement
SE 2	**STRUCTURAL OVERLAY - COMPOSITE FIBERS**	**Materials:**	Concrete Reinforced Masonry, Unreinforced Masonry

Description

Thin glass or carbon fibers woven into a fabric sheet can be applied to the surface of the wall to enhance the stiffness and strength of the wall. The fibers are generally applied to the surface using an epoxy resin binder and can be oriented in one direction or two directions. The composite fibers are used as tension reinforcing for the wall and can therefore increase the in-plane and out-of-plane strength of the wall.

Repair Materials

The typical repair methods use:

- Carbon-fiber or glass-fiber sheets
- Epoxy for bonding the sheets to the wall
- Anchors for attaching composite fiber sheets to substrate
- Surface coatings

Equipment

- Surface preparation equipment such as light chipping hammers or sandblasting equipment
- Brushes or rollers are used to apply the epoxy to the wall and to the fabric

Execution

Cracks in the walls should be repaired using epoxy or grout injection. Spalls should also be repaired. The wall surfaces are then prepared by lightly sandblasting the surface to the finish required by the manufacturer of the composite fiber.

A thin epoxy binding coat is applied to the surface using rollers. The composite fibers are saturated in epoxy and are pressed into the binder epoxy with a roller. The number of layers and the orientation of the layers depends on the design requirements. Additional epoxy may be applied to fully coat the fibers.

The fabric layers should wrap around the edges of the wall for a distance as recommended by the manufacturer. If a physical interference prevents wrapping the fabric, anchors should be installed through the fabric along the perimeter of the wall and secured to the substrate. The epoxy is then allowed to cure for at least 24 hours, or as recommended by the manufacturer.

After the epoxy has cured, the wall should be covered with a nonstructural coating such as paint, plaster, or wallboard. Special fire-resistant coatings are also available, if needed.

Quality Assurance

The behavior of the wall following application of the fiber reinforcement is strongly influenced by the procedures used to apply the composite fibers to the wall. The installation should be carefully monitored to verify that the work is being done in accordance with the manufacturer's recommendations.

REPAIR GUIDE
continued

The following items should be checked:

- The surface preparation of the wall to verify that all finishes and loose materials have been removed

- The mixing of the epoxy to verify that the two components have been mixed with the proper proportions

- The installed composite fabric to verify that the fabric has been completely embedded in the epoxy resin

- The overlapping of the fabric sheets and the wrapping of the sheets around corners, to verify that the sheets are anchored as required by the manufacturer

- The curing of the epoxy to ensure conformance with the manufacturer's recommendations

Limitations

There are no standards for the design of composite fibers used for the repair of shear walls. Manufacturers of the material can supply references and recommendations for application.

Carbon fibers have a modulus of elasticity and tensile strength that are greater than those of steel. Glass fibers have a lower modulus of elasticity and tensile strength. Both the glass and the carbon fibers exhibit brittle behavior in tension. The failure of the composite fiber system for out-of-plane loading is generally precipitated by debonding of the coating from the wall. Following the debonding, the composite fibers fail in a brittle manner (Reinhorn and Madan, 1995).

When composite fibers are installed in an area that requires a fire rating, a supplemental coating will need to be applied to prevent the epoxy from releasing dangerous fumes when heated.

References

Ehsani, M.R. and H Saadatmanesh, 1997, "Fiber Composites: An Economical Alternative for Retrofitting Earthquake-Damaged Precast-Concrete Walls", *Earthquake Spectra*, Vol. 13, No. 2, Earthquake Engineering Research Institute, Oakland, California, pp 225-241.

Laursen, P.T., F. Seible, G.A. Hegemier, and D. Innamorato, 1995, "Seismic Retrofit and Repair of Masonry Walls with Carbon Overlays", *Non-Metallic (FRP) Reinforcement for Concrete Structures*, RILEM, E & FN Spon, London, pp 619-623.

Reinhorn, A. M. and A. Madan, 1995, *Evaluation of Tyfo-S Fiber Wrap System For Out of Plane Strengthening of Masonry Walls*, Preliminary Test Report, Report No. AMR 95-0001, State University of New York at Buffalo.

REPAIR GUIDE	Repair Type:	Structural Enhancement
CRACK STITCHING	Materials:	Concrete
SE 3		Reinforced Masonry

Description

When a crack occurs in a lightly-reinforced concrete or reinforced masonry wall, the shear capacity along the crack can be restored and improved by local repair along the crack. This type of repair is most useful for sliding-shear behavior modes when reinforcing bars may be bent or the condition of the crack prevents epoxy from producing an adequate bond. For this repair, new reinforcing bars are inserted across the crack for improved shear resistance.

Repair Materials

- Reinforcing bars
- Epoxy for binding the reinforcing bars to the concrete or masonry

Equipment

The following equipment is needed:

- Rotary drill to create the holes (Core drills are not recommended)
- Air compressor and brushes
- Mixing and placing equipment for epoxy resin

Execution

Holes are drilled across the crack. The holes should be deep enough to develop the strength of the reinforcing bars in the wall and in the substrate above or below. Typically No. 4 or 5 bars are used with a hole depth equal to 18 inches on each side of the crack (ACI, 1994). The holes should intersect the crack at approximately a 45 degree angle. The spacing of the holes and the size of the reinforcing bars should be chosen to provide shear resistance using shear-friction theory for reinforcement inclined to the shear plane, in accordance with ACI 318.

The holes should be thoroughly cleaned by alternate use of compressed air and a brush. Epoxy is placed in the hole and then the reinforcing bar is inserted into the hole. Enough epoxy should be placed in the hole so that some epoxy is forced out of the hole when the reinforcing bar is placed.

Quality Assurance

The bond of the epoxy to the reinforcing bars and the substrate are critical to the effectiveness of the repair. For the bond to the substrate to be adequate, the hole must be thoroughly cleaned. This usually involves several cycles of brushing and blowing out the hole. The compressor used for blowing out the hole should be fitted with a filter to prevent oil from mixing with the air. The compressor oil will reduce the bond, if present. Water in the hole can also prevent proper bonding.

The reinforcing bar should not be rotated while it is inserted into the hole. Rotating the bar will break some of the initial bond of the epoxy, which can prevent further bonding.

An inspector should check each hole to verify that it has been adequately cleaned and of the required depth before inserting the reinforcing bar. Each hole should also be inspected following insertion of the bar to verify that the epoxy completely fills the annular space around the bar.

Limitations

Inserting dowels across the cracks is only effective if there is sufficient thickness of material above or below the wall to develop the bars. Using bars larger than No. 5 is not usually feasible, since drill bits may not be readily available to achieve the depth of the hole required to develop these larger bars.

Care must be taken to avoid damaging the existing reinforcing bars when drilling the holes for the new reinforcing bars. Rebar detectors should be used to lay out the existing bar placement.

Angle drilling with a rotary bit may be difficult to accomplish precisely by hand. A rig or guide may be needed to confirm that the hole is drilled at the proper angle.

References

ACI Committee 224, 1994, "Causes, Evaluation, and Repair of Cracks in Concrete Structures," ACI 224.1R-93, *ACI Manual of Concrete Practice*, American Concrete Institute, Detroit Michigan

Glossary

Component
A structural member such as a beam, column, or wall that is an individual part of a structural element

Cosmetic repairs
Repairs that improve the visual appearance of damage to a component. These repairs may also restore the nonstructural properties of the component, such as weather protection. Any structural benefit is negligible.

Damaging ground motion
The ground motion that shook the building under consideration and caused resulting damage. This ground motion may or may not have been recorded at the site of the building. In some cases, it may be an estimate of the actual ground motion that occurred. It might consist of estimated time-history records or corresponding response spectra.

Direct method
The determination of performance restoration measures from the observed damage without relative performance analysis.

Element
An assembly of structural components (e.g., coupled shear walls, frames)

Global displacement capacity
The maximum global displacement tolerable for a specific performance level. This global displacement limit is normally controlled by the acceptability of distortion of individual components or a group of components within the structure.

Global displacement demand
The overall displacement of a representative point on a building subject to a performance ground motion. The representative point is normally taken at the roof level or at the effective center of mass for a given mode of vibration.

Global structure
The assembly representing all of the structural elements of a building.

Infilled frame
A concrete or steel frame with concrete or masonry panels installed between the beams and columns

Nonlinear static procedure
A structural analysis technique in which the structure is modeled as an assembly of components capable of nonlinear force-displacement behavior and subjected to a monotonically increasing lateral load in a specific pattern to generate a global force-displacement capacity curve. The displacement demand is determined with a spectral representation of ground motion, using one of several alternative methods

Performance ground motion
Hypothetical ground motion consistent with the specified seismic hazard level associated with a specific performance objective. This is characterized by time-history record(s) or corresponding response spectra.

Performance index The ratio of the global displacement performance limit to the global displacement demand for a specific seismic performance objective. If this ratio is greater than 1.0, the seismic performance objective is satisfied. This index represents the degree to which the performance meets or falls short of the specific performance objective.

Performance level A hypothetical damage state for a building used to establish design seismic performance objectives. The most common performance levels, in order of decreasing amounts of damage, are collapse prevention, life safety, and immediate occupancy.

Performance loss 1.0 minus the ratio of the performance index for a damaged building to the performance index in its undamaged state for a specific performance objective. Performance loss ranges from 0 to 1.0 and represents the fraction of seismic performance that was lost during a damaging earthquake.

Performance objective A goal consisting of a specific performance level for a building subject to specific seismic hazard.

Performance restoration measures Actions that might be implemented for a damaged building that result in future performance equivalent to that of the building in its pre-event state for a specific performance objective. These hypothetical repairs would result in a restored performance index equal to the performance index of the undamaged building.

Pre-existing condition Physical evidence of inelastic deformation, damage, or deterioration of a structural component that existed before a damaging earthquake

Relative performance analysis An analysis of a building in its damaged and pre-event condition to determine the effects of the damage on the ability of the building to meet specific performance objectives

Repair An action taken to address a damaged building component.

Restoration The repair of structural components intended to restore the seismic performance of a damaged building to a level equivalent to the pre-event condition of the building.

Severity of damage The relative intensity of damage to a particular component, classified as insignificant, slight, moderate, heavy, or extreme.

Shear wall A concrete or masonry panel that is connected to the adjacent floor system or a surrounding frame (infilled frame) and that resists in-plane lateral loads.

Structural enhancements Repairs that comprise supplemental additions to, or removal and replacement of existing damaged components. They also include the addition of new components in the structure not necessarily at the site of existing damaged components. The intention is to replace rather than restore structural properties of damaged components.

Structural repairs Repairs that address damage to components to directly restore structural properties

Upgrade The repair of structural components intended to improve the seismic performance of a damaged building to a level better than that of the pre-event building.

Symbols

d_c Global displacement capacity for pre-event structure for specified performance level

d_c' Global displacement capacity for damaged structure for specified performance level

d_c^* Global displacement capacity for repaired structure for specified performance level

d_d Global displacement demand for pre-event structure for specified seismic hazard

d_d' Global displacement demand for damaged structure for specified seismic hazard

d_d^* Global displacement demand for repaired structure for specified seismic hazard

d_e Maximum global displacement caused by a damaging ground motion

References

ATC, 1989, *Procedures for the Post Earthquake Safety Evaluation of Buildings*, Applied Technology Council, ATC-20 Report, Redwood City, California.

ATC, 1995, *Addendum to the ATC-20 Post Earthquake Building Safety Evaluation Procedures*, Applied Technology Council, ATC-20-2 Report, Redwood City, California.

ATC, 1996, *Seismic Evaluation and Retrofit of Concrete Buildings,* prepared for the California Seismic Safety Commission by the Applied Technology Council, ATC-40 report, Redwood City, California.

ATC, 1997a, *NEHRP Guidelines for the Seismic Rehabilitation of Buildings*, prepared by the Applied Technology Council (ATC-33 project) for the Building Seismic Safety Council, published by the Federal Emergency Management Agency, Report No. FEMA 273, Washington, D.C.

ATC, 1997b, *NEHRP Commentary on the Guidelines for the Seismic Rehabilitation of Buildings*, prepared by the Applied Technology Council (ATC-33 project) for the Building Seismic Safety Council, published by the Federal Emergency Management Agency, Report No. FEMA 274, Washington, D.C.

ATC, 1998a, *Evaluation of Earthquake Damaged Concrete and Masonry Wall Buildings - Basic Procedures Manual*, prepared by the Applied Technology Council (ATC-43 project) for the Partnership for Response and Recovery, publisned by the Federal Emergency Management Agency, Report No. FEMA 306, Washington, D.C.

ATC, 1998b, *Evaluation of Earthquake Damaged Concrete and Masonry Wall Buildings - Technical Resources*, prepared by the Applied Technology Council (ATC-43 project) for the Partnership for Response and Recovery, publisned by the Federal Emergency Management Agency, Report No. FEMA 307, Washington, D.C.

ATC, in preparation, *Earthquake Loss Evaluation Methodology and Databases for Utah*, Applied Technology Council, ATC-36 report, Redwood City, California.

City of Los Angeles, 1985, *City of Los Angeles Building Code, Division 88 - Earthquake Hazard Reduction in Existing Buildings*, Los Angeles, California.

City and County of San Francisco, 1989, *City and County of San Francisco Municipal Code: Building Code*, Book Publishing Company, Seattle, Washington.

CSSC, 1994, *Compendium of Background Reports on the Northridge Earthquake for Executive Order W-78-94*, California Seismic Safety Commission (Report No. SSC 94-08).

Hanson, R.D., 1996, "The Evaluation of Reinforced Concrete Members Damaged by Earthquakes," *Spectra*, Vol. 12, No. 3, Earthquake Engineering Research Institute, Oakland, California.

Holmes, W.T., 1994, "Policies and Standards for Reoccupancy Repair of Earthquake Damaged Buildings," *Spectra*, Vol. 10, No. 1, Earthquake Engineering Research Institute, Oakland, California.

ICBO, 1997 and other years, *Uniform Building Code*, International Conference of Building Officials, Whittier, California.

NIBS, 1997, *Earthquake Loss Estimation Methodology: HAZUS 97*, prepared by National Institute of Building Standards, NIBS Document Number 5200, for the Federal Emergency Management Agency, Washington, D.C.

Olson, R.S., and Olson, R.A., 1992, *"But the Rubble's Standing Up": The Politics of Building Safety in Oroville, California 1975-1976*, VSP Associates, Sacramento, California.

Russell, J.E., 1994, "Post Earthquake Reconstruction Regulation by Local Government," *Spectra*, Vol. 10, No. 1, Earthquake Engineering Research Institute, Oakland, California.

Sugano, S., 1996, "State-of-the-Art in Techniques for Rehabilitation of Buildings," *Proceedings of the Eleventh World Conference on Earthquake Engineering*, Acapulco, Mexico.

ATC-43 Project Participants

Atc Management

Mr. Christopher Rojahn,
Principal Investigator
Applied Technology Council
555 Twin Dolphin Drive, Suite 550
Redwood City, CA 94065

Mr. Craig Comartin,
Co-PI and Project Director
7683 Andrea Avenue
Stockton, CA 95207

Technical Management Committee

Prof. Dan Abrams
University of Illinois
1245 Newmark Civil Eng'g. Lab., MC 250
205 North Mathews Avenue
Urbana, IL 61801-2397

Mr. James Hill
James A. Hill & Associates, Inc.
1349 East 28th Street
Signal Hill, CA 90806

Mr. Andrew T. Merovich
A.T. Merovich & Associates, Inc.
1163 Francisco Blvd., Second Floor
San Rafael, CA 94901

Prof. Jack Moehle
Earthquake Engineering Research Center
University of California at Berkeley
1301 South 46th Street
Richmond, CA 94804

FEMA/PARR Representatives

Mr. Timothy McCormick
PaRR Representative
Dewberry & Davis
8401 Arlington Boulevard
Fairfax, VA 22031-4666

Mr. Mark Doroudian
PaRR Representative
42 Silkwood
Aliso Viejo, CA 92656

Prof. Robert D. Hanson
FEMA Technical Monitor
74 North Pasadena Avenue, CA-1009-DR
Parsons Bldg., West Annex, Room 308
Pasadena, CA 91103

Materials Working Group

Dr. Joe Maffei, Group Leader
c/o Rutherford & Chekene
303 Second Street, Suite 800 North
San Francisco, CA 94107

Mr. Brian Kehoe, Lead Consultant
Wiss, Janney, Elstner Associates, Inc.
2200 Powell Street, Suite 925
Emeryville, CA 94608

Dr. Greg Kingsley
KL&A of Colorado
805 14th Street
Golden, CO 80401

Mr. Bret Lizundia
Rutherford & Chekene
303 Second Street, Suite 800 North
San Francisco, CA 94107

Prof. John Mander
SUNY at Buffalo
Department of Civil Engineering
212 Ketter Hall
Buffalo, NY 14260

Analysis Working Group

Prof. Mark Aschheim, Group Leader
University of Illinois at Urbana
2118 Newmark CE Lab
205 North Mathews, MC 250
Urbana, IL 61801

Prof. Mete Sozen, Senior Consultant
Purdue University, School of Engineering
1284 Civil Engineering Building
West Lafayette, IN 47907-1284

Project Review Panel

Mr. Gregg J. Borchelt
Brick Institute of America
11490 Commerce Park Drive, #300
Reston, VA 20191

Dr. Gene Corley
Construction Technology Labs
5420 Old Orchard Road
Skokie, IL 60077-1030

Mr. Edwin Huston
Smith & Huston
Plaza 600 Building, 6th & Stewart, #620
Seattle, WA 98101

Prof. Richard E. Klingner
University of Texas
Civil Engineering Department
Cockbell Building, Room 4-2
Austin, TX 78705

Mr. Vilas Mujumdar
Office of Regulation Services
Division of State Architect
General Services
1300 I Street, Suite 800
Sacramento, CA 95814

Mr. Hassan A. Sassi
Governors Office of Emergency Services
74 North Pasadena Avenue
Pasadena, CA 91103

Mr. Carl Schulze
Libby Engineers
4452 Glacier Avenue
San Diego, CA 92120

Mr. Daniel Shapiro
SOH & Associates
550 Kearny Street, Suite 200
San Francisco, CA 94108

Prof. James K. Wight
University of Michigan
Department of Civil Engineering
2368 G G Brown
Ann Arbor, MI 48109-2125

Mr. Eugene Zeller
Long Beach Department of Building & Safety
333 W. Ocean Boulevard, Fourth Floor
Long Beach, CA 90802

Applied Technology Council Projects And Report Information

One of the primary purposes of Applied Technology Council is to develop resource documents that translate and summarize useful information to practicing engineers. This includes the development of guidelines and manuals, as well as the development of research recommendations for specific areas determined by the profession. ATC is not a code development organization, although several of the ATC project reports serve as resource documents for the development of codes, standards and specifications.

Applied Technology Council conducts projects that meet the following criteria:

1. The primary audience or benefactor is the design practitioner in structural engineering.

2. A cross section or consensus of engineering opinion is required to be obtained and presented by a neutral source.

3. The project fosters the advancement of structural engineering practice.

A brief description of several major completed projects and reports is given in the following section. Funding for projects is obtained from government agencies and tax-deductible contributions from the private sector.

ATC-1: This project resulted in five papers that were published as part of *Building Practices for Disaster Mitigation, Building Science Series 46*, proceedings of a workshop sponsored by the National Science Foundation (NSF) and the National Bureau of Standards (NBS). Available through the National Technical Information Service (NTIS), 5285 Port Royal Road, Springfield, VA 22151, as NTIS report No. COM-73-50188.

ATC-2: The report, *An Evaluation of a Response Spectrum Approach to Seismic Design of Buildings*, was funded by NSF and NBS and was conducted as part of the Cooperative Federal Program in Building Practices for Disaster Mitigation. Available through the ATC office. (Published 1974, 270 Pages)

ABSTRACT: This study evaluated the applicability and cost of the response spectrum approach to seis-

mic analysis and design that was proposed by various segments of the engineering profession. Specific building designs, design procedures and parameter values were evaluated for future application. Eleven existing buildings of varying dimensions were redesigned according to the procedures.

ATC-3: The report, *Tentative Provisions for the Development of Seismic Regulations for Buildings* (ATC-3-06), was funded by NSF and NBS. The second printing of this report, which includes proposed amendments, is available through the ATC office. (Published 1978, amended 1982, 505 pages plus proposed amendments)

ABSTRACT: The tentative provisions in this document represent the results of a concerted effort by a multi-disciplinary team of 85 nationally recognized experts in earthquake engineering. The provisions serve as the basis for the seismic provisions of the 1988 *Uniform Building Code* and the 1988 and subsequent issues of the *NEHRP Recommended Provisions for the Development of Seismic Regulation for New Buildings*. The second printing of this document contains proposed amendments prepared by a joint committee of the Building Seismic Safety Council (BSSC) and the NBS.

ATC-3-2: The project, Comparative Test Designs of Buildings Using ATC-3-06 Tentative Provisions, was funded by NSF. The project consisted of a study to develop and plan a program for making comparative test designs of the ATC-3-06 Tentative Provisions. The project report was written to be used by the Building Seismic Safety Council in its refinement of the ATC-3-06 Tentative Provisions.

ATC-3-4: The report, *Redesign of Three Multistory Buildings: A Comparison Using ATC-3-06 and 1982 Uniform Building Code Design Provisions*, was published under a grant from NSF. Available through the ATC office. (Published 1984, 112 pages)

ABSTRACT: This report evaluates the cost and technical impact of using the 1978 ATC-3-06 report, *Tentative Provisions for the Development of Seismic Regulations for Buildings*, as amended by a joint committee of the Building Seismic Safety Council and the National Bureau of Standards in 1982. The evaluations are based on studies of three existing California buildings redesigned in accordance with the ATC-3-06 Tentative Provisions and the 1982 *Uniform Building Code*. Included in the report are recommendations to code implementing bodies.

ATC-3-5: This project, Assistance for First Phase of ATC-3-06 Trial Design Program Being Conducted by the Building Seismic Safety Council, was funded by the Building Seismic Safety Council to provide the services of the ATC Senior Consultant and other ATC personnel to assist the BSSC in the conduct of the first phase of its Trial Design Program. The first phase provided for trial designs conducted for buildings in Los Angeles, Seattle, Phoenix, and Memphis.

ATC-3-6: This project, Assistance for Second Phase of ATC-3-06 Trial Design Program Being Conducted by the Building Seismic Safety Council, was funded by the Building Seismic Safety Council to provide the services of the ATC Senior Consultant and other ATC personnel to assist the BSSC in the conduct of the second phase of its Trial Design Program. The second phase provided for trial designs conducted for buildings in New York, Chicago, St. Louis, Charleston, and Fort Worth.

ATC-4: The report, *A Methodology for Seismic Design and Construction of Single-Family Dwellings*, was published under a contract with the Department of Housing and Urban Development (HUD). Available through the ATC office. (Published 1976, 576 pages)

ABSTRACT: This report presents the results of an in-depth effort to develop design and construction details for single-family residences that minimize the potential economic loss and life-loss risk associated with earthquakes. The report: (1) discusses the ways structures behave when subjected to seismic forces, (2) sets forth suggested design criteria for conventional layouts of dwellings constructed with conventional materials, (3) presents construction details that do not require the designer to perform analytical calculations, (4) suggests procedures for efficient plan-checking, and (5) presents recommendations including details and schedules for use in the field by construction personnel and building inspectors.

ATC-4-1: The report, *The Home Builders Guide for Earthquake Design*, was published under a contract with HUD. Available through the ATC office. (Published 1980, 57 pages)

ABSTRACT: This report is an abridged version of the ATC-4 report. The concise, easily understood text of the Guide is supplemented with illustrations and 46 construction details. The details are provided to ensure that houses contain structural features that are properly positioned, dimensioned and constructed to resist earthquake forces. A brief description is included on how earthquake forces impact on houses and some precautionary constraints are given with respect to site selection and architectural designs.

ATC-5: The report, *Guidelines for Seismic Design and Construction of Single-Story Masonry Dwellings in Seismic Zone 2*, was developed under a contract with HUD. Available through the ATC office. (Published 1986, 38 pages)

ABSTRACT: The report offers a concise methodology for the earthquake design and construction of single-story masonry dwellings in Seismic Zone 2 of the United States, as defined by the 1973 *Uniform Building Code*. The Guidelines are based in part on shaking table tests of masonry construction conducted at the University of California at Berkeley Earthquake Engineering Research Center. The report is written in simple language and includes basic house plans, wall evaluations, detail drawings, and material specifications.

ATC-6: The report, *Seismic Design Guidelines for Highway Bridges*, was published under a contract with the Federal Highway Administration (FHWA). Available through the ATC office. (Published 1981, 210 pages)

ABSTRACT: The Guidelines are the recommendations of a team of sixteen nationally recognized experts that included consulting engineers, academics, state and federal agency representatives from throughout the United States. The Guidelines embody several new concepts that were significant departures from then existing design provisions. Included in the Guidelines are an extensive commentary, an example demonstrating the use of the

Guidelines, and summary reports on 21 bridges redesigned in accordance with the Guidelines. The guidelines have been adopted by the American Association of Highway and Transportation Officials as a guide specification.

ATC-6-1: The report, *Proceedings of a Workshop on Earthquake Resistance of Highway Bridges*, was published under a grant from NSF. Available through the ATC office. (Published 1979, 625 pages)

ABSTRACT: The report includes 23 state-of-the-art and state-of-practice papers on earthquake resistance of highway bridges. Seven of the twenty-three papers were authored by participants from Japan, New Zealand and Portugal. The Proceedings also contain recommendations for future research that were developed by the 45 workshop participants.

ATC-6-2: The report, *Seismic Retrofitting Guidelines for Highway Bridges*, was published under a contract with FHWA. Available through the ATC office. (Published 1983, 220 pages)

ABSTRACT: The Guidelines are the recommendations of a team of thirteen nationally recognized experts that included consulting engineers, academics, state highway engineers, and federal agency representatives. The Guidelines, applicable for use in all parts of the United States, include a preliminary screening procedure, methods for evaluating an existing bridge in detail, and potential retrofitting measures for the most common seismic deficiencies. Also included are special design requirements for various retrofitting measures.

ATC-7: The report, *Guidelines for the Design of Horizontal Wood Diaphragms*, was published under a grant from NSF. Available through the ATC office. (Published 1981, 190 pages)

ABSTRACT: Guidelines are presented for designing roof and floor systems so these can function as horizontal diaphragms in a lateral force resisting system. Analytical procedures, connection details and design examples are included in the Guidelines.

ATC-7-1: The report, *Proceedings of a Workshop of Design of Horizontal Wood Diaphragms*, was

published under a grant from NSF. Available through the ATC office. (Published 1980, 302 pages)

ABSTRACT: The report includes seven papers on state-of-the-practice and two papers on recent research. Also included are recommendations for future research that were developed by the 35 workshop participants.

ATC-8: This report, *Proceedings of a Workshop on the Design of Prefabricated Concrete Buildings for Earthquake Loads*, was funded by NSF. Available through the ATC office. (Published 1981, 400 pages)

ABSTRACT: The report includes eighteen state-of-the-art papers and six summary papers. Also included are recommendations for future research that were developed by the 43 workshop participants.

ATC-9: The report, *An Evaluation of the Imperial County Services Building Earthquake Response and Associated Damage*, was published under a grant from NSF. Available through the ATC office. (Published 1984, 231 pages)

ABSTRACT: The report presents the results of an in-depth evaluation of the Imperial County Services Building, a 6-story reinforced concrete frame and shear wall building severely damaged by the October 15, 1979 Imperial Valley, California, earthquake. The report contains a review and evaluation of earthquake damage to the building; a review and evaluation of the seismic design; a comparison of the requirements of various building codes as they relate to the building; and conclusions and recommendations pertaining to future building code provisions and future research needs.

ATC-10: This report, *An Investigation of the Correlation Between Earthquake Ground Motion and Building Performance*, was funded by the U.S. Geological Survey (USGS). Available through the ATC office. (Published 1982, 114 pages)

ABSTRACT: The report contains an in-depth analytical evaluation of the ultimate or limit capacity of selected representative building framing types, a discussion of the factors affecting the seismic performance of buildings, and a summary and comparison of seismic design and seismic risk parameters currently in widespread use.

ATC-10-1: This report, *Critical Aspects of Earthquake Ground Motion and Building Damage Potential*, was co-funded by the USGS and the NSF. Available through the ATC office. (Published 1984, 259 pages)

ABSTRACT: This document contains 19 state-of-the-art papers on ground motion, structural response, and structural design issues presented by prominent engineers and earth scientists in an ATC seminar. The main theme of the papers is to identify the critical aspects of ground motion and building performance that currently are not being considered in building design. The report also contains conclusions and recommendations of working groups convened after the Seminar.

ATC-11: The report, *Seismic Resistance of Reinforced Concrete Shear Walls and Frame Joints: Implications of Recent Research for Design Engineers*, was published under a grant from NSF. Available through the ATC office. (Published 1983, 184 pages)

ABSTRACT: This document presents the results of an in-depth review and synthesis of research reports pertaining to cyclic loading of reinforced concrete shear walls and cyclic loading of joint reinforced concrete frames. More than 125 research reports published since 1971 are reviewed and evaluated in this report. The preparation of the report included a consensus process involving numerous experienced design professionals from throughout the United States. The report contains reviews of current and past design practices, summaries of research developments, and in-depth discussions of design implications of recent research results.

ATC-12: This report, *Comparison of United States and New Zealand Seismic Design Practices for Highway Bridges*, was published under a grant from NSF. Available through the ATC office. (Published 1982, 270 pages)

ABSTRACT: The report contains summaries of all aspects and innovative design procedures used in New Zealand as well as comparison of United States and New Zealand design practice. Also included are research recommendations developed

at a 3-day workshop in New Zealand attended by 16 U.S. and 35 New Zealand bridge design engineers and researchers.

ATC-12-1: This report, *Proceedings of Second Joint U.S.-New Zealand Workshop on Seismic Resistance of Highway Bridges*, was published under a grant from NSF. Available through the ATC office. (Published 1986, 272 pages)

ABSTRACT: This report contains written versions of the papers presented at this 1985 Workshop as well as a list and prioritization of workshop recommendations. Included are summaries of research projects being conducted in both countries as well as state-of-the-practice papers on various aspects of design practice. Topics discussed include bridge design philosophy and loadings; design of columns, footings, piles, abutments and retaining structures; geotechnical aspects of foundation design; seismic analysis techniques; seismic retrofitting; case studies using base isolation; strong-motion data acquisition and interpretation; and testing of bridge components and bridge systems.

ATC-13: The report, *Earthquake Damage Evaluation Data for California*, was developed under a contract with the Federal Emergency Management Agency (FEMA). Available through the ATC office. (Published 1985, 492 pages)

ABSTRACT: This report presents expert-opinion earthquake damage and loss estimates for industrial, commercial, residential, utility and transportation facilities in California. Included are damage probability matrices for 78 classes of structures and estimates of time required to restore damaged facilities to pre-earthquake usability. The report also describes the inventory information essential for estimating economic losses and the methodology used to develop loss estimates on a regional basis.

ATC-14: The report, *Evaluating the Seismic Resistance of Existing Buildings*, was developed under a grant from the NSF. Available through the ATC office. (Published 1987, 370 pages)

ABSTRACT: This report, written for practicing structural engineers, describes a methodology for performing preliminary and detailed building seismic evaluations. The report contains a state-of-practice review; seismic loading criteria; data collection procedures; a detailed description of the building classification system; preliminary and detailed analysis procedures; and example case studies, including nonstructural considerations.

ATC-15: The report, *Comparison of Seismic Design Practices in the United States and Japan*, was published under a grant from NSF. Available through the ATC office. (Published 1984, 317 pages)

ABSTRACT: The report contains detailed technical papers describing design practices in the United States and Japan as well as recommendations emanating from a joint U.S.-Japan workshop held in Hawaii in March, 1984. Included are detailed descriptions of new seismic design methods for buildings in Japan and case studies of the design of specific buildings (in both countries). The report also contains an overview of the history and objectives of the Japan Structural Consultants Association.

ATC-15-1: The report, *Proceedings of Second U.S.-Japan Workshop on Improvement of Building Seismic Design and Construction Practices*, was published under a grant from NSF. Available through the ATC office. (Published 1987, 412 pages)

ABSTRACT: This report contains 23 technical papers presented at this San Francisco workshop in August, 1986, by practitioners and researchers from the U.S. and Japan. Included are state-of-the-practice papers and case studies of actual building designs and information on regulatory, contractual, and licensing issues.

ATC-15-2: The report, *Proceedings of Third U.S.-Japan Workshop on Improvement of Building Structural Design and Construction Practices*, was published jointly by ATC and the Japan Structural Consultants Association. Available through the ATC office. (Published 1989, 358 pages)

ABSTRACT: This report contains 21 technical papers presented at this Tokyo, Japan, workshop in July, 1988, by practitioners and researchers from the U.S., Japan, China, and New Zealand. Included are state-of-the-practice papers on various topics,

including braced steel frame buildings, beam-column joints in reinforced concrete buildings, summaries of comparative U. S. and Japanese design, and base isolation and passive energy dissipation devices.

ATC-15-3: The report, *Proceedings of Fourth U.S.-Japan Workshop on Improvement of Building Structural Design and Construction Practices*, was published jointly by ATC and the Japan Structural Consultants Association. Available through the ATC office. (Published 1992, 484 pages)

ABSTRACT: This report contains 22 technical papers presented at this Kailua-Kona, Hawaii, workshop in August, 1990, by practitioners and researchers from the United States, Japan, and Peru. Included are papers on postearthquake building damage assessment; acceptable earth-quake damage; repair and retrofit of earthquake damaged buildings; base-isolated buildings, including Architectural Institute of Japan recommendations for design; active damping systems; wind-resistant design; and summaries of working group conclusions and recommendations.

ATC-15-4: The report, *Proceedings of Fifth U.S.-Japan Workshop on Improvement of Building Structural Design and Construction Practices*, was published jointly by ATC and the Japan Structural Consultants Association. Available through the ATC office. (Published 1994, 360 pages)

ABSTRACT: This report contains 20 technical papers presented at this San Diego, California workshop in September, 1992. Included are papers on performance goals/acceptable damage in seismic design; seismic design procedures and case studies; construction influences on design; seismic isolation and passive energy dissipation; design of irregular structures; seismic evaluation, repair and upgrading; quality control for design and construction; and summaries of working group discussions and recommendations.

ATC-16: This project, Development of a 5-Year Plan for Reducing the Earthquake Hazards Posed by Existing Nonfederal Buildings, was funded by FEMA and was conducted by a joint venture of ATC, the Building Seismic Safety Council and the Earthquake Engineering

Research Institute. The project involved a workshop in Phoenix, Arizona, where approximately 50 earthquake specialists met to identify the major tasks and goals for reducing the earthquake hazards posed by existing non-federal buildings nationwide. The plan was developed on the basis of nine issue papers presented at the workshop and workshop working group discussions. The Workshop Proceedings and Five-Year Plan are available through the Federal Emergency Management Agency, 500 "C" Street, S.W., Washington, DC 20472.

ATC-17: This report, *Proceedings of a Seminar and Workshop on Base Isolation and Passive Energy Dissipation*, was published under a grant from NSF. Available through the ATC office. (Published 1986, 478 pages)

ABSTRACT: The report contains 42 papers describing the state-of-the-art and state-of-the-practice in base-isolation and passive energy-dissipation technology. Included are papers describing case studies in the United States, applications and developments worldwide, recent innovations in technology development, and structural and ground motion issues. Also included is a proposed 5-year research agenda that addresses the following specific issues: (1) strong ground motion; (2) design criteria; (3) materials, quality control, and long-term reliability; (4) life cycle cost methodology; and (5) system response.

ATC-17-1: This report, *Proceedings of a Seminar on Seismic Isolation, Passive Energy Dissipation and Active Control*, was published under a grant from NSF. Available through the ATC office. (Published 1993, 841 pages)

ABSTRACT: The 2-volume report documents 70 technical papers presented during a two-day seminar in San Francisco in early 1993. Included are invited theme papers and competitively selected papers on issues related to seismic isolation systems, passive energy dissipation systems, active control systems and hybrid systems.

ATC-18: The report, *Seismic Design Criteria for Bridges and Other Highway Structures: Current and Future*, was published under a contract from the Multi-disciplinary Center for Earthquake Engineering Research (formerly NCEER), with funding from the Federal Highway Administration. Available through the ATC office. (Published 1997, 152 pages)

ABSTRACT: This report documents the findings of a 4-year project to review and assess current seismic design criteria for new highway construction. The report addresses performance criteria, importance classification, definitions of seismic hazard for areas where damaging earthquakes have longer return periods, design ground motion, duration effects, site effects, structural response modification factors, ductility demand, design procedures, foundation and abutment modeling, soil-structure interaction, seat widths, joint details and detailing reinforced concrete for limited ductility in areas with low-to-moderate seismic activity. The report also provides lengthy discussion on future directions for code development and recommended research and development topics.

ATC-19: The report, *Structural Response Modification Factors* was funded by NSF and NCEER. Available through the ATC office. (Published 1995, 70 pages)

ABSTRACT: This report addresses structural response modification factors (R factors), which are used to reduce the seismic forces associated with elastic response to obtain design forces. The report documents the basis for current R values, how R factors are used for seismic design in other countries, a rational means for decomposing R into key components, a framework (and methods) for evaluating the key components of R, and the research necessary to improve the reliability of engineered construction designed using R factors.

ATC-20: The report, *Procedures for Postearthquake Safety Evaluation of Buildings*, was developed under a contract from the California Office of Emergency Services (OES), California Office of Statewide Health Planning and Development (OSHPD) and FEMA. Available through the ATC office (Published 1989, 152 pages)

ABSTRACT: This report provides procedures and guidelines for making on-the-spot evaluations and decisions regarding continued use and occupancy of earthquake damaged buildings. Written specifically for volunteer structural engineers and building inspectors, the report includes rapid and detailed evaluation procedures for inspecting buildings and posting them as "inspected" (apparently safe), "limited entry" or "unsafe". Also included are special procedures for evaluation of essential buildings (e.g., hospitals), and evaluation procedures for non-structural elements, and geotechnical hazards.

ATC-20-1: The report, *Field Manual: Postearthquake Safety Evaluation of Buildings*, was developed under a contract from OES and OSHPD. Available through the ATC office (Published 1989, 114 pages)

> ABSTRACT: This report, a companion Field Manual for the ATC-20 report, summarizes the postearthquake safety evaluation procedures in brief concise format designed for ease of use in the field.

ATC-20-2: The report, *Addendum to the ATC-20 Postearthquake Building Safety Procedures* was published under a grant from the NSF and funded by the USGS. Available through the ATC office. (Published 1995, 94 pages)

> ABSTRACT: This report provides updated assessment forms, placards, and procedures that are based on an in-depth review and evaluation of the widespread application of the ATC-20 procedures following five earthquakes occurring since the initial release of the ATC-20 report in 1989.

ATC-20-3: The report, *Case Studies in Rapid Postearthquake Safety Evaluation of Buildings*, was funded by ATC and R. P. Gallagher Associates. Available through the ATC office. (Published 1996, 295 pages)

> ABSTRACT: This report contains 53 case studies using the ATC-20 Rapid Evaluation procedure. Each case study is illustrated with photos and describes how a building was inspected and evaluated for life safety, and includes a completed safety assessment form and placard. The report is intended to be used as a training and reference manual for building officials, building inspectors, civil and structural engineers, architects, disaster workers, and others who may be asked to perform safety evaluations after an earthquake.

ATC-20-T: The report, *Postearthquake Safety Evaluation of Buildings Training Manual* was developed under

a contract with FEMA. Available through the ATC office. (Published 1993, 177 pages; 160 slides)

> ABSTRACT: This training manual is intended to facilitate the presentation of the contents of the ATC-20 and ATC-20-1. The training materials consist of 160 slides of photographs, schematic drawings and textual information and a companion training presentation narrative coordinated with the slides. Topics covered include: posting system; evaluation procedures; structural basics; wood frame, masonry, concrete, and steel frame structures; nonstructural elements; geotechnical hazards; hazardous materials; and field safety.

ATC-21: The report, *Rapid Visual Screening of Buildings for Potential Seismic Hazards: A Handbook*, was developed under a contract from FEMA. Available through the ATC office. (Published 1988, 185 pages)

> ABSTRACT: This report describes a rapid visual screening procedure for identifying those buildings that might pose serious risk of loss of life and injury, or of severe curtailment of community services, in case of a damaging earthquake. The screening procedure utilizes a methodology based on a "sidewalk survey" approach that involves identification of the primary structural load resisting system and building materials, and assignment of a basic structural hazards score and performance modification factors based on observed building characteristics. Application of the methodology identifies those buildings that are potentially hazardous and should be analyzed in more detail by a professional engineer experienced in seismic design.

ATC-21-1: The report, *Rapid Visual Screening of Buildings for Potential Seismic Hazards: Supporting Documentation*, was developed under a contract from FEMA. Available through the ATC office. (Published 1988, 137 pages)

> ABSTRACT: Included in this report are (1) a review and evaluation of existing procedures; (2) a listing of attributes considered ideal for a rapid visual screening procedure; and (3) a technical discussion of the recommended rapid visual screening procedure that is documented in the ATC-21 report.

ATC-21-2: The report, *Earthquake Damaged Buildings: An Overview of Heavy Debris and Victim Extrication*, was developed under a contract from FEMA. (Published 1988, 95 pages)

> ABSTRACT: Included in this report, a companion volume to the ATC-21 and ATC-21-1 reports, is state-of-the-art information on (1) the identification of those buildings that might collapse and trap victims in debris or generate debris of such a size that its handling would require special or heavy lifting equipment; (2) guidance in identifying these types of buildings, on the basis of their major exterior features, and (3) the types and life capacities of equipment required to remove the heavy portion of the debris that might result from the collapse of such buildings.

ATC-21-T: The report, *Rapid Visual Screening of Buildings for Potential Seismic Hazards Training Manual* was developed under a contract with FEMA. Available through the ATC office. (Published 1996, 135 pages; 120 slides)

> ABSTRACT: This training manual is intended to facilitate the presentation of the contents of the ATC-21 report. The training materials consist of 120 slides and a companion training presentation narrative coordinated with the slides. Topics covered include: description of procedure, building behavior, building types, building scores, occupancy and falling hazards, and implementation.

ATC-22: The report, *A Handbook for Seismic Evaluation of Existing Buildings (Preliminary)*, was developed under a contract from FEMA. Available through the ATC office. (Originally published in 1989; revised by BSSC and published as the *NEHRP Handbook for Seismic Evaluation of Existing Buildings* in 1992, 211 pages)

> ABSTRACT: This handbook provides a methodology for seismic evaluation of existing buildings of different types and occupancies in areas of different seismicity throughout the United States. The methodology, which has been field tested in several programs nationwide, utilizes the information and procedures developed for and documented in the ATC-14 report. The handbook includes checklists, diagrams, and sketches designed to assist the user.

ATC-22-1: The report, *Seismic Evaluation of Existing Buildings: Supporting Documentation*, was developed under a contract from FEMA. (Published 1989, 160 pages)

> ABSTRACT: Included in this report, a companion volume to the ATC-22 report, are (1) a review and evaluation of existing buildings seismic evaluation methodologies; (2) results from field tests of the ATC-14 methodology; and (3) summaries of evaluations of ATC-14 conducted by the National Center for Earthquake Engineering Research (State University of New York at Buffalo) and the City of San Francisco.

ATC-23A: The report, *General Acute Care Hospital Earthquake Survivability Inventory for California, Part A: Survey Description, Summary of Results, Data Analysis and Interpretation*, was developed under a contract from the Office of Statewide Health Planning and Development (OSHPD), State of California. Available through the ATC office. (Published 1991, 58 pages)

> ABSTRACT: This report summarizes results from a seismic survey of 490 California acute care hospitals. Included are a description of the survey procedures and data collected, a summary of the data, and an illustrative discussion of data analysis and interpretation that has been provided to demonstrate potential applications of the ATC-23 database.

ATC-23B: The report, *General Acute Care Hospital Earthquake Survivability Inventory for California, Part B: Raw Data*, is a companion document to the ATC-23A Report and was developed under the above-mentioned contract from OSHPD. Available through the ATC office. (Published 1991, 377 pages)

> ABSTRACT: Included in this report are tabulations of raw general site and building data for 490 acute care hospitals in California.

ATC-24: The report, *Guidelines for Seismic Testing of Components of Steel Structures*, was jointly funded by the American Iron and Steel Institute (AISI), American Institute of Steel Construction (AISC), National Center for Earthquake Engineering Research (NCEER), and NSF. Available through the ATC office. (Published 1992, 57 pages)

ABSTRACT: This report provides guidance for most cyclic experiments on components of steel structures for the purpose of consistency in experimental procedures. The report contains recommendations and companion commentary pertaining to loading histories, presentation of test results, and other aspects of experimentation. The recommendations are written specifically for experiments with slow cyclic load application.

ATC-25: The report, *Seismic Vulnerability and Impact of Disruption of Lifelines in the Conterminous United States*, was developed under a contract from FEMA. Available through the ATC office. (Published 1991, 440 pages)

ABSTRACT: Documented in this report is a national overview of lifeline seismic vulnerability and impact of disruption. Lifelines considered include electric systems, water systems, transportation systems, gas and liquid fuel supply systems, and emergency service facilities (hospitals, fire and police stations). Vulnerability estimates and impacts developed are presented in terms of estimated first approximation direct damage losses and indirect economic losses.

ATC-25-1: The report, *A Model Methodology for Assessment of Seismic Vulnerability and Impact of Disruption of Water Supply Systems*, was developed under a contract from FEMA. Available through the ATC office. (Published 1992, 147 pages)

ABSTRACT: This report contains a practical methodology for the detailed assessment of seismic vulnerability and impact of disruption of water supply systems. The methodology has been designed for use by water system operators. Application of the methodology enables the user to develop estimates of direct damage to system components and the time required to restore damaged facilities to pre-earthquake usability. Suggested measures for mitigation of seismic hazards are also provided.

ATC-28: The report, *Development of Recommended Guidelines for Seismic Strengthening of Existing Buildings, Phase I: Issues Identification and Resolution*, was developed under a contract with FEMA. Available through the ATC office. (Published 1992, 150 pages)

ABSTRACT: This report identifies and provides resolutions for issues that will affect the development of guidelines for the seismic strengthening of existing buildings. Issues addressed include: implementation and format, coordination with other efforts, legal and political, social, economic, historic buildings, research and technology, seismicity and mapping, engineering philosophy and goals, issues related to the development of specific provisions, and nonstructural element issues.

ATC-29: The report, *Proceedings of a Seminar and Workshop on Seismic Design and Performance of Equipment and Nonstructural Elements in Buildings and Industrial Structures*, was developed under a grant from NCEER and NSF. Available through the ATC office. (Published 1992, 470 pages)

ABSTRACT: These Proceedings contain 35 papers describing state-of-the-art technical information pertaining to the seismic design and performance of equipment and nonstructural elements in buildings and industrial structures. The papers were presented at a seminar in Irvine, California in 1990. Included are papers describing current practice, codes and regulations; earthquake performance; analytical and experimental investigations; development of new seismic qualification methods; and research, practice, and code development needs for specific elements and systems. The report also includes a summary of a proposed 5-year research agenda for NCEER.

ATC-29-1: The report, *Proceedings Of Seminar On Seismic Design, Retrofit, And Performance Of Nonstructural Components*, was developed under a grant from NCEER and NSF. Available through the ATC office. (Published 1998, 518 pages)

ABSTRACT: These Proceedings contain 38 papers presenting current research, practice, and informed thinking pertinent to seismic design, retrofit, and performance of nonstructural components. The papers were presented at a seminar in San Francisco, California, in 1998. Included are papers describing observed performance in recent earthquakes; seismic design codes, standards, and procedures for commercial and institutional buildings; seismic design issues relating to industrial and hazardous material facilities; design, analysis, and testing; and seismic evaluation and rehabilitation of conventional and essential facilities, including hospitals.

ATC-30: The report, *Proceedings of Workshop for Utilization of Research on Engineering and Socioeconomic Aspects of 1985 Chile and Mexico Earthquakes*, was developed under a grant from the NSF. Available through the ATC office. (Published 1991, 113 pages)

ABSTRACT: This report documents the findings of a 1990 technology transfer workshop in San Diego, California, co-sponsored by ATC and the Earthquake Engineering Research Institute. Included in the report are invited papers and working group recommendations on geotechnical issues, structural response issues, architectural and urban design considerations, emergency response planning, search and rescue, and reconstruction policy issues.

ATC-31: The report, *Evaluation of the Performance of Seismically Retrofitted Buildings*, was developed under a contract from the National Institute of Standards and Technology (NIST, formerly NBS) and funded by the USGS. Available through the ATC office. (Published 1992, 75 pages)

ABSTRACT: This report summarizes the results from an investigation of the effectiveness of 229 seismically retrofitted buildings, primarily unreinforced masonry and concrete tilt-up buildings. All buildings were located in the areas affected by the 1987 Whittier Narrows, California, and 1989 Loma Prieta, California, earthquakes.

ATC-32: The report, *Improved Seismic Design Criteria for California Bridges: Provisional Recommendations*, was funded by the California Department of Transportation (Caltrans). Available through the ATC office. (Published 1996, 215 Pages)

ABSTRACT: This report provides recommended revisions to the current *Caltrans Bridge Design Specifications* (BDS) pertaining to seismic loading, structural response analysis, and component design. Special attention is given to design issues related to reinforced concrete components, steel components, foundations, and conventional bearings. The recommendations are based on recent research in the field of bridge seismic design and the performance

of Caltrans-designed bridges in the 1989 Loma Prieta and other recent California earthquakes.

ATC-34: The report, *A Critical Review of Current Approaches to Earthquake Resistant Design*, was developed under a grant from NCEER and NSF. Available through the ATC office. (Published, 1995, 94 pages)

ABSTRACT. This report documents the history of U. S. codes and standards of practice, focusing primarily on the strengths and deficiencies of current code approaches. Issues addressed include: seismic hazard analysis, earthquake collateral hazards, performance objectives, redundancy and configuration, response modification factors (R factors), simplified analysis procedures, modeling of structural components, foundation design, nonstructural component design, and risk and reliability. The report also identifies goals that a new seismic code should achieve.

ATC-35: This report, *Enhancing the Transfer of U.S. Geological Survey Research Results into Engineering Practice* was developed under a contract with the USGS. Available through the ATC office. (Published 1996, 120 pages)

ABSTRACT: The report provides a program of recommended "technology transfer" activities for the USGS; included are recommendations pertaining to management actions, communications with practicing engineers, and research activities to enhance development and transfer of information that is vital to engineering practice.

ATC-35-1: The report, *Proceedings of Seminar on New Developments in Earthquake Ground Motion Estimation and Implications for Engineering Design Practice*, was developed under a cooperative agreement with USGS. Available through the ATC office. (Published 1994, 478 pages)

ABSTRACT: These Proceedings contain 22 technical papers describing state-of-the-art information on regional earthquake risk (focused on five specific regions--California, Pacific Northwest, Central United States, and northeastern North America); new techniques for estimating strong ground motions as a function of earthquake source, travel path, and site parameters; and new developments specifically applicable to geotechnical engineering and the seismic design of buildings and bridges.

ATC-37: The report, *Review of Seismic Research Results on Existing Buildings,* was developed in conjunction with the Structural Engineers Association of California and California Universities for Research in Earthquake Engineering under a contract from the California Seismic Safety Commission (SSC). Available through the Seismic Safety Commission as Report SSC 94-03. (Published, 1994, 492 pages)

ABSTRACT. This report describes the state of knowledge of the earthquake performance of nonductile concrete frame, shear wall, and infilled buildings. Included are summaries of 90 recent research efforts with key results and conclusions in a simple, easy-to-access format written for practicing design professionals.

ATC-40: The report, *Seismic Evaluation and Retrofit of Concrete Buildings,* was developed under a contract from the California Seismic Safety Commission. Available through the ATC office. (Published, 1996, 612 pages)

ABSTRACT. This 2-volume report provides a state-of-the-art methodology for the seismic evaluation and retrofit of concrete buildings. Specific guidance is provided on the following topics: performance objectives; seismic hazard; determination of deficiencies; retrofit strategies; quality assurance procedures; nonlinear static analysis procedures; modeling rules; foundation effects; response limits; and nonstructural components. In 1997 this report received the Western States Seismic Policy Council "Overall Excellence and New Technology Award."

ATC-44: The report, *Hurricane Fran, South Carolina, September 5, 1996: Reconnaissance Report,* is available through the ATC office. (Published 1997, 36 pages.)

ABSTRACT: This report represents ATC's expanded mandate into structural engineering problems arising from wind storms and coastal flooding. It contains information on the causative hurricane; coastal impacts, including storm surge, waves, structural forces and erosion; building codes; observations and interpretations of damage; and lifeline performance. Conclusions address man-made beach nourishment, the effects of missile-like debris, breaches in the sandy barrier islands, and the timing and duration of such investigations.

ATC-R-1: The report, *Cyclic Testing of Narrow Plywood Shear Walls,* was developed with funding from the Henry J. Degenkolb Memorial Endowment Fund of the Applied Technology Council. Available through the ATC office (Published 1995, 64 pages)

ABSTRACT: This report documents ATC's first self-directed research program: a series of static and dynamic tests of narrow plywood wall panels having the standard 3.5-to-1 height-to-width ratio and anchored to the sill plate using typical bolted, 9-inch, 5000-lb. capacity hold-down devices. The report provides a description of the testing program and a summary of results, including comparisons of drift ratios found during testing with those specified in the seismic provisions of the 1991 *Uniform Building Code.*

Applied Technology Council
Sponsors, Supporters, and Contributors

Sponsors

Structural Engineers Association of California
James R. & Sharon K. Cagley
John M. Coil
Burkett & Wong

Supporters

Charles H. Thornton
Degenkolb Engineers
Japan Structural Consultants Association

Contributors

Lawrence D. Reaveley
Omar Dario Cardona Arboleda
Edwin T. Huston
John C. Theiss
Reaveley Engineers
Rutherford & Chekene
E. W. Blanch Co.

www.ingramcontent.com/pod-product-compliance
Lightning Source LLC
Chambersburg PA
CBHW080519290526
45790CB00006B/2237